York's Other Churches and Chapels

by

Bryan Seymour

The Church's restoration
In eighteen-eighty-three
Has left for contemplation
Not what there used to be ...

John Betjeman: Hymn

Highgate Publications (Beverley) Limited, 1992

For
Horace John and Kathleen Mary
who have made this, and so
much else, possible.

Published by Highgate Publications (Beverley) Limited
24 Wylies Road, Beverley, North Humberside, HU17 7AP
Telephone (0482) 866826

Printed by BA Press
Unit 7, Tokenspire Park, Woodmansey, Beverley
North Humberside, HU17 0TB
Telephone (0482) 882232

ISBN 0 948929 55 3

British Library Cataloguing in Publication Data
Seymour, Bryan John
  York's Other Churches and Chapels
  I. Title
  726.50942843
ISBN 0-948929-55-3

Contents

Front Cover:

York College for Girls Chapel: Gabriel — Stained glass	*Unitarian Chapel St. Saviourgate: Cast-iron gates*	*St. Wilfred's Roman Catholic Church: Tower*	*Central Methodist Church: Flashed glass*
All Saints, Pavement: Door ring			*St. Martin-le-Grand: Clock*
All Saints, Pavement: Lantern tower	*Central Methodist Church: Portico*	*All Saints, North Street: the Resurrection — Stained glass*	*Priory Street Baptist Chapel: Interior*

Back Cover:

St. Columba's United Reformed Church, Priory Street	*St. Michael-le-Belfrey: East window detail*	*St. John's Church: Arts Centre*
St. Saviour's Church Archaelogical Resource Centre		*St. Michael's Church, Spurriergate: Door case*
All Saints, North Street: Angel-Chancel roof		*St. Columba's United Reformed Church: front interior*
St. Michael-le-Belfrey: Sanctuary	*St. Michael's Church, Spurriergate: Clock face*	*Assembly of God*

St. Martin-le-Grand:
The clock in Coney Street.

St. Cuthbert, Peasholme Green:
St. Cuthbert with the head of King Oswald.

iii

Acknowledgements

I am most grateful to the following who made time to write, phone, open closed doors and conduct me round their places of worship:

E. Burnett and E. Simmonds (Society of Friends, York)

W. Webster (Society of Friends, Kirkby Moorside)

Mr. L. Creed (formerly Warden, St. Sampson's)

Mr. S. White (St. George's)

Miss M. Green (Church Warden, St. Helen and St. Martin-le-Grand)

Mr. P. Hulbert (Church Warden, All Saints Pavement, with St. Crux)

Pastors K. and R. Hall (Assembly of God)

The Revd. I. Collins (Baptist Church)

The Revd. D. Mullins (Central Methodist Chapel)

The Revd. S. H. Knight (Unitarian Chapel)

Mr. B. Giles (Kingdom Hall of Jehovah's Witnesses)

Mrs. C. Hutchinson (St. Mary, Bishophill Junior)

Staff at St. Cuthbert's Administrative Centre

Mrs. J. A. Dalgarno (School Secretary, York College for Girls)

Mr. D. Tyson (Verger, St. Michael-le-Belfrey)

The following have generously allowed me to use their illustrations:

Mrs. A. Watson (photograph of Revd. D. Watson)

Mr. Bailey Oliver (photograph at dedication of St. George's)

York Minster Library (reproductions of Tate Wilkinson, J. P. Pritchett, William Richardson, St. Martin-le-Grand and the former Chapel of the Archbishop's Palace)

Permission to take photographs was given by the clergy and ministers mentioned above and:

Miss S. Wilkinson (Spurriergate Centre)

Mr. J. Bowles (Redundant Churches Fund)

Mr. N. Johns (Custodian, Holy Trinity, Goodramgate)

Mgr. S. Kilbane (St. George's)

The Revds. T. Preston (St. Denys), A. Hodge (St. Olave's), Dr. G. Higginson (Holy Trinity, Micklegate), Canon J. Armstrong (All Saints, Pavement), D. Porter (All Saints, Pavement), C. Puckrin (St. Michael-le-Belfrey), E. Jones (All Saints, North Street), J. Corker (St. Helen's), M. Marsden (St. Wilfrid's)

The Elders of York Kingdom Hall of Jehovah's Witnesses

Mr. J. Wheatley, Clerk of the Company of Merchant Adventurers of the City of York.

York Archaeological Trust

Mrs. J. L. Clare, Headmistress, York College for Girls.

The Director (Dr. A. Hodges) and Deputy Director (Mrs. H. Durrant) Castle Museum, York

Samuel Smith's Brewery, Tadcaster

I have also received information and assistance from:

Mr. R. Barr (Sub-Librarian) and Mr. C. McCarter (York Minster Library)

Miss J. Pinder (Civic Secretary, Mansion House)

Mr. D. Robertson (North Yorkshire Co-operative Funeral Service)

Mr. M. Tucker

The Revds. O. Beckerlegge and R. Carberry

To all of whom I tender my thanks.

B. J. Seymour
Nether Poppleton, York
January, 1992

The extracts from Sir John Betjeman's *Church Poems* are quoted with permission of John Murray (Publishers) Ltd.

Left for Contemplation

In late medieval times York had more than 40 churches within its walls; only Norwich and the City of London had more. Some 20 remain although half of these are no longer in use as places of worship.

Since the last quarter of the 17th century there have been added two Roman Catholic churches and 25 Nonconformist places of worship, of which nine have totally disappeared and eight have had a change of use.

The 20th century has added one Roman Catholic shrine, a Kingdom Hall of Jehovah's Witnesses and an Anglican school chapel to the city's sacred places.

So there are 'left for contemplation' 20 former places of worship now serving the community and its visitors in many and various ways, and rather more functioning as they were intended to — left for contemplation, praise and glory of God — even if no longer always at the service of the denominations which built them.

Christian people — indeed others, too — will ponder the wastefulness and the unremitting financial burdens which the upkeep of so many buildings place on congregations — buildings used, in many cases, comparatively so little and by so few. Of course, the multiplicity and diversity of so many places of worship bear witness to the varieties of religious experience within, and the richness of, the Christian tradition, as well as being visible tokens of the scandalous divisions within the Body of Christ which present such a profoundly confusing and conflicting picture to non-Christians. That said, York's places of worship, past and present, provide residents and visitors alike with a wealth of interest, pleasure and refreshment (both physical and spiritual) and if, after all the changes they have gone through, there is 'left ... not what there used to be' this is nothing new, however much a matter of nostalgic regret. 'Change and decay in much around I see ...' (if the hymn may be slightly adapted) but there is also much to be thankful for in the handsome restorations and imaginative new uses found for so many buildings, the loss of which would ruin the endangered City of York. In fact conservation and preservation are flourishing activities and for these an enormous debt of gratitude is owed to such bodies as the Civic Trust and the Redundant Churches Fund, as well as to individual congregations and benefactors.

A. Churches and Chapels in regular use
  (i) Roman Catholic:
       St. George
       St. Wilfrid
       ⋆St. Margaret Clitherow

  (ii) Anglican:
       ⋆All Saints, North Street
       ⋆St. Denys
       ⋆St. Helen
       ⋆Holy Trinity, Micklegate
       ⋆St. Martin-le-Grand
       ⋆St. Mary, Bishophill Junior
       ⋆St. Michael-le-Belfrey
       ⋆St. Olave
       ⋆The Cathedral and Metropolitical Church of St. Peter in York
       York College for Girls Chapel

  Occasional services at:
       ⋆Holy Trinity, Goodramgate
       ⋆Trinity Chapel, Merchant Adventurers' Hall

  (iii) Nonconformist:
       ⋆St. Andrew
       Assembly of God
       Central Methodist Chapel
       St. Columba (United Reformed Church)
       Elim Pentecostal Church
       Friends Meeting House
       York Baptist Church
       Unitarian Chapel
       Victoria Bar Chapel
       Kingdom Hall of Jehovah's Witnesses

⋆Medieval building

1

B. Churches and Chapels disused and converted

Church of Christ, Cromwell Road
    (Chapel of Rest)
Lendal Congregational Chapel (Restaurant)
Ebenezer Chapel (Printers)
*St. John, Micklegate (Arts Centre)
*St. Martin-cum-Gregory
    (Diocesan Mothers' Union Centre)
Peasholme Green Chapel (Dental Surgery)
*St. Michael, Spurriergate
    (Spurriergate Centre)
Monk Bar Chapel
    (Shops; Judges' and Bailiffs' Rooms)
*St. Sampson (Old People's Centre)
*St. Saviour
    (Archaeological Resource Centre)
'Room in Pump Yard' (Offices)
Trinity Chapel, Peckitt Street
    (part of Fire Station)
St. George's Chapel, Walmgate
    (Builders' Store) ·
*St. Mary's Abbey Church (ruins)
*Chapel of former Archbishop's Palace
    (York Minster Library)
*Chapel of St. Anthony's Hall
    (Borthwick Institute)
*Bedern Chapel (Store)
Skeldergate Mission
    (empty, awaiting redevelopment)

*Medieval building

St. Margaret, Walmgate.

Scope of This Book

The aim of this book is to give a brief introduction to the numerous places of worship within the walls of the City of York, other than the Minster.

An exception has been made, by the inclusion of St. Olave's Church, Marygate, which is strictly speaking *outside* the city walls but within the walls of St. Mary's Abbey.

With regret, therefore, St. Lawrence's, Hull Road, and the Salvation Army Citadel in Gillygate are omitted although both are within a (very good thrower's) stone's throw of the walls, and the latter is about to undergo a major restoration and refurbishment at the time of writing.

In addition to the places of worship in current use, redundant churches and chapels have been included; some of these have been put to new uses, such as St. Sampson's and the Peasholme Green Chapel. No attempt has been made to trace all the non-purpose-built meeting places.

As far as possible the more abstruse technicalities of architectural historians have been avoided and the reader will not be burdened with all the complex and confusing details of the development of the buildings listed here. Most York churches have been mutilated and modified, allowed to decay and then renovated and restored out of all recognition several times in the course of their history, so that what is seen today is a fascinating mixture of the medieval, the Victorian and the 20th-century. Chapels, and meeting houses too, rarely survive as originally envisaged. A number needed extension with the addition of galleries quite soon after their construction; the tendency in the present century has been to diminish seating provision, if not to abandon the buildings entirely in favour of chapels in more convenient locations.

NOTE ON ORIENTATION: where is east?

It is a widely-held opinion that old churches in England were built on a east/west axis, so that the main altar in the sanctuary was at the east end of the chancel, and the main entrance or, more often, the tower at the western end of the nave.

Reasons offered for this arrangement are varied: some claim that a pre-Christian practice of facing the rising sun is the origin, others, that the Christian holy places connected with the birth, life, death, and resurrection of Jesus Christ are in the east and therefore Christians in their worship face in that direction whence came their religion. (The parallel in Judaism is obvious — Jews arrange their synagogues so that the cupboard containing the sacred scrolls of the Jewish Law and Prophets is at the end of the building nearest Jerusalem and the site of the Temple. Moslems, too, pray facing the direction of their holy city of Mecca.)

In York, however, as in many ancient towns and cities, not all churches are so orientated. The Minster, it is true, is built on the east/west axis but this lies outside the scope of this book. About eight of the parish churches are approximately on the east/west line, but almost as many are more nearly south-east/north-west and three are almost north-east/south-west. Despite this, for the sake of convenience throughout this book, the convention followed elsewhere, is adopted, which assumes that the end of the church at which the main altar is situated is in the east, so that to left and right of this altar are north and south respectively and the 'back' of the church is in the west.

The foregoing does not apply to the Nonconformist places of worship.

East/west axis	South-east/North-west
All Saints, North Street	St. John, Micklegate
All Saints, Pavement	St. Margaret
St. Cuthbert	St. Martin-le-Grand
St. Denys	St. Martin-cum-Gregory
St. Helen	St. Michael-le-Belfrey
St. Mary, Castlegate	St. Sampson
Holy Trinity, Micklegate	St. Saviour

North-east/South-west

St. Mary, Bishophill Junior
St. Michael, Spurriergate
St. Olave

NOTE ON BUILDING MATERIALS

The medieval churches are built largely of limestone, probably from the Tadcaster area, as are the City walls and York Minster. The roofs are of timber, covered usually with tiles or slates, and, occasionally, lead. Some of the churches — *e.g.* St. Martin-cum-Gregory and St. Mary, Bishophill Junior — incorporate re-used Roman stone. Several towers were re-built in the 17th century (or later) in brick — *e.g.* St. John, Micklegate, and St. Margaret, Walmgate. Brick was also used extensively in the restoration of St. Andrew's. The 20th-century anchorage at All Saints, North Street is an early example of the use of concrete with half-timber cladding.

The earliest Nonconformist chapels which survive were built entirely of brick — the Unitarian Chapel (originally Presbyterian) in St. Saviourgate and its near neighbour, the former Peasholme Green Chapel (Methodist). The former now has a slate roof and the latter pantiles.

Later chapels also were of brick — the so-called 'red and white brick' which is often grey, buff and purplish as well. Stone dressings and terracotta are also frequently found. Stone was only used on a large scale on the frontage of the imposing Central Methodist Chapel (neo-Classical) and Priory Street Baptist Chapel (neo-Gothic). White brick was chosen for St. Columba's Presbyterian (now United Reformed) Church and red brick for the former Wesley Chapel.

The 19th-century Roman Catholic churches have used yellow Bradford wall-stone and red Cumbrian sandstone at St. Wilfrid's and limestone at St. George's. Both have slate roofs, as have the Nonconformist chapels of similar date.

GENERAL CHARACTERISTICS

The Medieval Churches

In the main, York churches have nave and north and south aisles of equal length, without an eastern chancel or sanctuary extension. The ground plan, therefore, is rectangular, and the customary divisions between nave, chancel and sanctuary, if they survive, are marked by screens and/or steps. The tower, usually at the west end of the nave in York, is frequently 'engaged' — *i.e.* its base falls within the rectangular plan of the church. These characteristics are probably explained by the limitations of space, although the eastern ends of some churches have been modified — notably All Saints, Pavement and St. Michael's, Spurriergate.

Similarly surrounding churchyards have become vestigial in many places, or have disappeared altogether, in the interests of road widening or other 'improvement'. St. John's, Micklegate, lost its graveyard in the transformation of the 50s and what remains of St. Michael's, Spurriergate, is hidden away behind the building. St. Helen's churchyard was paved to make St. Helen's Square.

Square-based towers with octagonal upper parts are found at All Saints, Pavement, St. Mary's, Castlegate and All Saints, North Street (the two latter surmounted by slender spires). The pierced octagonal lantern of All Saints has clearly been the model for the western turrets of St. Michael-le-Belfrey and St. Helen's.

York churches contain a wealth of splendid woodwork of the 17th and 18th centuries. Altar pieces displaying the Lord's Prayer, the Ten Commandments and the Creed bear witness to the fact that 'literacy was almost as rife as it is today' (in Sir John Betjeman's vivid phrase) and these were often accompanied by excellent three-sided altar railings with a semi-circular gate at the centre, used, it is said, by the officiant at marriage services. Notable examples are in St. Michael's, Spurriergate, St. Martin-cum-Gregory, Holy Trinity, Goodramgate, and St. Michael-le-Belfrey (where the Commandments have been replaced by a painting of the Nativity).

Seventeenth-century pulpits, too, are prominent, the best at All Saints, Pavement (1634) and St. Martin-cum-Gregory (1636), the latter church also having a fine poor box, charity boards and bread shelf.

The Anglican emphasis on the Word *and* the Sacraments (*i.e.* of Holy Communion and Baptism) is thus maintained. Mayoral boards and bequest boards as well as carved and painted royal arms abound.

Most of the City's churches have some interesting and ancient stained glass, surviving both the Reformation and the Civil War thanks to Sir Thomas Fairfax. St. Denys, Walmgate, has the oldest surviving glass in a York parish church (13th-century), All Saints, North Street, perhaps the most interesting (14th and 15th-centuries) although St. Michael-le-Belfrey and St. Michael's, Spurriergate, could challenge that claim. St. Martin-cum-Gregory has rare 18th-century glass by the Peckitt family and several churches including St. Helen's, All Saints, Pavement and Holy Trinity, Micklegate, have good 19th-century glass. Only a small amount of 20th-century glass has risked comparison with the superb medieval windows — tiny windows in Holy Trinity, Micklegate, St. Olave's, York College for Girls Chapel and a larger one in St. Martin-le-Grand, which also boasts the largest single 15th-century window outside the Minster.

Memorials are numerous in most of the Anglican churches, commemorating the well-to-do and the erstwhile famous who could not gain post-mortuary access to the noblest resting places in the Minster. It should, perhaps, be made clear that a memorial is no evidence of an actual tomb, and certainly not of the precise location of the remains of the departed, as monuments have often a somewhat eventful history and are far from being the immutable remembrances their donors hoped for.

Ledger stones (memorial slabs on the floors of churches) are often the most difficult to locate and frequently far from easy to decipher after centuries of wear. The best collection in St. Martin-cum-Gregory is the easiest to see as the pews have been removed from this redundant church. Brasses, if not lost, stolen or strayed, are frequently re-positioned on walls (as in St. Michael's, Spurriergate, All Saints, North Street, St. Mary's, Castlegate and All Saints, Pavement). A few really spectacular monuments call for special notice: those of 18th-century Robert and Priscilla Squire (he was M.P. for Scarborough) classically elegant in St. Michael-le-Belfrey, and 17th-century Lord Mayor Robert Watter with wife and family in highly coloured repose in St. Crux. Indeed, St. Crux, although only a church room now, has a remarkable collection of handsomely restored wall tablets rescued from the demolished church of St. Crux. It includes at least one delightful memorial by Fisher of York to Henry Waite who died in 1780. The Fishers were a family firm who were obviously the first choice when memorials were required by the prosperous of Georgian York. St. Michael's, Spurriergate has another (to William Hutchinson who died in 1772) — 'one of Fisher's finest works' according to Hutchinson and Palliser in their *Bartholomew's Guide*. The inscription notes:

> A partiality for the place of his Birth
> in which he had lived eighty nine years
> led him to diftinguifh by his Will
> the RECTOR and the POOR of this Parifh
> with a legacy
> of three Hundred Pounds.

One wonders if the Rector was pleased to be so 'diftinguifhed'.

The fonts of York's churches are unremarkable, unless St. Helen's amalgam of lovely late 12th-century bowl on an inverted 15th-century capital over a 13th-century base appeals. St. Cuthbert's early 19th-century cast-iron font, painted green, was a rarity (but probably not very lovable). At all events it has been removed. However, the importance of the font in Anglican thought is equal to that of the altar (these being the places at which the two 'dominical' sacraments are administered) and several churches are the proud possessors of first-rate font covers, mostly early 18th-century work. The best is probably St. Martin-le-

Grand's (1717) but those in the other St. Martin's and Holy Trinity, Micklegate, are worth a visit. The 1963 font cover by George Pace in St. Olave's is a worthy successor.

The Nonconformist Chapels

The Nonconformist chapels in York, with the exception of the Unitarians' (originally Presbyterian 1692), which is cruciform, are rectangular in plan even if the addition of classrooms, offices, vestries and so forth, obscures the basic simplicity. The Central Methodist Chapel is not quite rectangular, the corners distant from St. Saviourgate having been rounded off. This chapel, like the now demolished Salem Chapel, has a classical facade on a grand scale. Other City chapels of the 19th century are also based on Renaissance styles although the Priory Street Baptist Chapel risked a Gothic Revival design, the effect of which is somewhat diminished by the removal of the tower which once dominated Priory Street.

Salem Chapel by J. P. Prichett
from an early 19th-century engraving.

The typical chapel interior here in York, as elsewhere, was and is so arranged that the maximum number of worshippers could be seated in a relatively small space in order that everyone had a good view of, and the opportunity to hear, the preacher in the pulpit.

The emphasis on the preaching of the Word of God is still made clear in these buildings, even if pulpits are lowered (or sometimes disused) and other furnishings have become more prominent of late.

In a number of chapels screens and overhead projectors are in evidence, making the same point by these 20th-century means of communication as did the enormous pulpits of highly polished and superbly worked wood.

To seat the greatest number economically under one roof, galleries were from early times introduced into chapels. These are usually situated on the three sides of the chapel, leaving the fourth for the pulpit — with the organ sited behind and above. If the gallery extends across the fourth side this is usually reserved for a choir. Such galleries are usually supported on slender cast-iron columns, sometimes surmounted by Corinthian capitals, with minimum visual impedance.

The organ came to be an essential part of the chapel scene in the 19th century (as it did in churches) and the singing of hymns played (and plays) an important part in Nonconformist worship. The organ at the Central Methodist Chapel is notable and the handsome organ cases in other chapels still preside over the worship throughout the City — even if electronic keyboards, percussion and wind instruments, together with the paraphernalia of amplification, are *de rigueur* for late-20th-century congregations.

Fonts are usually small and portable in Nonconformist chapels which do not practise immersion; those that do (for example the Baptists and the Assembly of God) share facilities using the baptistery in front of the pulpit in the Baptist Chapel.

Communion tables are almost always found at ground floor level, at the front of the chapel, below the pulpit. The table used for the Lord's Supper is a piece of good quality furniture — no more and no less — and, although now sometimes decorated with a bowl of flowers or even a brass cross, has nothing of the importance given to the altar in Roman Catholic and Anglican churches. The relative unimportance (or at any rate, infrequency) of the Lord's Supper which has been characteristic of some Nonconformist churches is, perhaps, becoming less extreme.

Monuments are not numerous in Nonconformist chapels. The exception to this is, again, the Unitarian Chapel which has a fine collection.

Some stained glass is to be found, notably in Priory Street chapels, and the St. Saviourgate chapels retain their flashed glass windows.

The Friends' Meeting House is simplicity itself: a well-proportioned room, the ceiling of which was lowered in recent re-building on the site. Ordinary furniture, a table with Bible and flowers, no stained glass or memorials — nothing to distract from the intention to worship in 'Spirit and in truth' by those who find outward and visible signs unhelpful.

Roman Catholic Churches

The two major Roman Catholic churches of York were built in the middle of the 19th century and both have served as cathedral churches of the short-lived diocese of Beverley.

Both of these churches are redolent of continental Catholicity in their internal features, and this is also true of the external appearance of St. Wilfrid's which is French Gothic in style.

Both have short chancel-sanctuaries (the organs and choir spaces being situated in western galleries) with high altars and elaborate tabernacles for the reserved Sacrament. Each church has one (or more) subsidiary altars and both have an altar which now stands, in accordance with modern liturgical practice, at the western end of the sanctuary. At St. George's this is no longer divided from the people by the altar rail which has been made into a handsome marble altar.

Each church has an excellent series of 14 Stations of the Cross (very different in style); the only comparable Anglican series is in St. Olave's.

Carving, statues and stained glass add colour and interest, and the elaborate surroundings of the principal altars lay emphasis on the importance of the Mass at the centre of Catholic worship.

Both churches have glazed narthexes, which serve a useful social function.

St. Margaret Clitherow's shrine in Shambles is a suitably furnished room in a medieval timber-framed house, purchased by the diocese of Middlesbrough in the 1950's.

CHURCH AND CHAPEL BUILDINGS IN YORK

It is known that by the beginning of the 4th century A.D. Christianity had reached York, for in 314 Bishop Eborius from York attended a Council at Arles, together with two other bishops from Britain. How and when the faith spread to this outpost of the Roman Empire is a matter for conjecture, as is the number of Christians there were in the city in those days. Soldiers or traders may have brought the new religion, before the Emperor Constantine embraced Christianity, but where the first believers worshipped is unknown. Perhaps the numbers were so few that gatherings took place in private houses as they commonly did elsewhere at this period. It is assumed that after the withdrawal of the Romans at the beginning of the 5th century Christianity dwindled and eventually died out, so that, when King Edwin of Northumbria married his Christian wife, Ethelburga from Kent, in 625, York was regarded as pagan territory. The advent of Ethelburga and her bishop Paulinus re-introduced the Christian faith to these parts, and the conversion of Edwin and other members of his family followed in 627, when the first Minster — a small wooden church — was erected for the baptism of the king. The location of that church, and the stone Minster which succeeded it, is unknown, so it is not surprising, perhaps, that no traces survive of any of the more humble places of worship which no doubt grew up in York during the 7th-10th centuries.

The earliest survival is the substantial tower of St. Mary, Bishophill Junior, which dates from the 11th (or possibly the 10th century) and which may have been the nave of the Anglo-Saxon church. The base of the tower has re-used Roman squared stones in it, as have other York churches; these were no doubt available in quantity and more readily accessible a thousand years ago than they are today. St. Cuthbert's is also a Saxon foundation, and a Saxon dedication stone believed to refer to St. Mary's, Castlegate, is preserved in 'The York Story'. St. Olave's, too, was founded before the Norman Conquest, but nothing remains of the original structure.

The Normans built a number of churches in the city, in addition to the huge Minster for Archbishop Thomas of Bayeux, but little survives the constant urge to modernise and extend which seems to have possessed our medieval forebears. Several Norman doorways have been preserved, notably in the Walmgate area, but none is *in situ*, and if they were not originally doorways at all but chancel arches, as has been suggested by some, the churches they belonged to must have been fairly small.

Most of the parish churches of the city date from the 13th-15th centuries, St. Michael-le-Belfrey alone from the early 16th century, but many have been rebuilt or enlarged several times and almost all were heavily 'restored' (if not actually re-built) in the last century. Prior to the Reformation of the 16th century these medieval churches were the centres of parish and gild life and furnished with many more altars and images than are found today. For example, St. Michael's, Spurriergate, had, besides its high altar, altars to Our Lady, St. John the Baptist, St. Margaret, the Holy Trinity, St. Anne, St. Mary Magdalen, St. Thomas and St. Nicholas as well as a Jesu altar. St. Mary's Abbey Church at the beginning of the 16th century had 11 altars in addition to the high altar, necessary when every priest was required to say a daily Mass, and when Masses for the souls of the departed were believed to aid their passage through purgatory. Images abounded. In St. Michael-le-Belfrey, for example, there were statues of St. Barbara, St. Paul, St. Anthony, St. Blaise, St. Erasmus, St. Osyth, Our Lady of Pity and the Salutation, and parishioners made bequests to enable lights to be maintained before such images, as well as before the Easter Sepulchre and the Blessed Sacrament. The devout also bequeathed other property to their parish churches (sometimes, perhaps, in the spirit in which some people today who do not know what to do with an unwanted picture, plant stand, piano or whatever, 'give it to God' — to the despair of those who seek to maintain standards of good taste in their churches). In 1440 Alice Samoure gave a 'red ark' (*i.e.* chest) to St. Denys' Church 'for the keeping of the goods of the said church' — such a chest is still kept in the church. Alice Croull in 1464 gave her blue bedspread to be laid before the high altar of St. Mary's, Castlegate, whenever there should be a need for it. In 1508 John Petty, Mayor, bequeathed to St. Helen's 'my jaket of velvet ... to mak thame a vestment, and if it be noght sufficient to make a vestment to take my velvet slevys to mak it owt.' Similarly a tile maker bequeathed 500 tiles for the roof of All Saints, North Street, in 1444. Yet, in spite of all this good will and parochial pride, reports on the condition of churches and their furnishings from the same period often make depressing reading. No wonder that after the Reformation the number of city churches was reduced from over 40 to about half that number, with the amalgamation of parishes *e.g.* St. Martin's, Micklegate with St. Gregory's (which had been further up the road). The intrepid Celia Fiennes visited York in 1697 and made disparaging comparisons between the City and some of the less salubrious parts of London, but noted — inaccurately, as it happens — 'there are a great many pretty Churches, 16 in number'. After the break with Rome the interiors of the surviving churches were stripped of their superfluous altars, the images of the saints were broken up, vestments sold and wall paintings white-washed out of existence. Glass, happily, in York at least, survived. Other changes also began to alter the appearance of churches in York (and throughout the land). In earlier times there was little or no provision made for people to sit down during services — only the weakest, the elderly, and the sick, 'went to the wall' where a stone ledge gave some support. With greater emphasis on reading the

Scriptures and expounding them in sermons the need to provide benches or pews was felt, and by the time of the Commonwealth (17th century) churches began to resemble Holy Trinity, Goodramgate. Pulpits became prominent and box pews and galleries filled all the available spaces. The 18th century introduced great classic altar pieces or reredoses, displaying the Creed, the Commandments and the Lord's Prayer; benefaction boards, royal arms and mayoral boards also make their appearance.

At the same time mural memorials in marble and other handsome stones begin to be fashionable. (Earlier, generally speaking, funerary monuments were either ledger stones on the floor of the church with incised lettering, or more vulnerable brasses set into the stone matrices.)

The process of amalgamation of parishes and the demolition of churches continued into the 19th and early 20th centuries. Demolition of St. Crux in the last century and Holy Trinity (or Christ Church) in what is now King's Square and St. Mary, Bishophill Senior, in this century may be the last of such devastation: redundant churches are now better cared-for and new uses found for them. St. John's, Micklegate, St. Mary's, Castlegate, St. Sampson's, St. Cuthbert's, St. Michael's, Spurriergate, and St. Saviour's have all been found new rôles and the buildings have been sympathetically and imaginatively restored and adapted.

The 19th century was also a time of modernisation for churches throughout the land and attempts were made to restore their medieval splendour. Galleries and box pews were banished, organs took over from more varied musical forces; varnished pine pews, encaustic tiles and a good deal of not very pleasing stained glass were inserted, and the kind of interiors we are accustomed to in many places today were established. Structurally the churches were often made sounder than they had been for years although Victorian roofs cause much concern a hundred years later. In York several churches were almost completely rebuilt and many were 'pruned' to allow for road 'improvements'.

One redundant church remains a museum piece to indicate what disappeared in the last century — Holy Trinity, Goodramgate — and another, St. Margaret's, is permanently closed (and used as a store, at present). One church only was damaged by enemy action in 1942 — St. Martin-le-Grand, Coney Street — and that has been partially restored and forms an attractive quiet zone in the heart of the shopping centre.

Our Churches are our history shown
In wood and glass and iron and stone.
John Betjeman: Churchyards

During the Commonwealth 1649-1660 the Anglican Church was suspended and Prayer Book worship forbidden. The church buildings in York were taken over by Presbyterians, Baptists and Congregationalists, and it was during this period that George Fox, founder of the Society of Friends (or Quakers) visited York and was ejected from the south door of the Minster (1651) for protesting at a sermon by the Presbyterian minister temporarily installed there. A meeting house was built by the Society of Friends in 1674 (this has not survived) but meetings had been held in a private house before this, as well as in York Castle where friends were sometimes imprisoned.

The first Nonconformist chapel is that of the Unitarians, built in St. Saviourgate in 1692 for the Presbyterians, under the patronage of Lady Sarah Hewley. This unusual building, one of the hundred most important Nonconformist chapels in the country, was originally surrounded by a high wall as the Presbyterians had suffered persecution in the 1680s.

The next century saw the birth of Methodism, and the Peasholme Green Chapel was built in 1759. John Wesley visited York many times. There was, of course, no break at first from the Church of England and Wesley's adherents would happily hear sermons at Peasholme Green Chapel and then walk up to St. Michael-le-Belfrey to receive Holy Communion, during the period of the Evangelical Revival. During the 19th century, Methodism became the leading Nonconformist denomination in York. The principal

Nonconformist chapels date from this time, Priory Street and St. Saviourgate being favoured sites for Methodists as well as Baptists and Presbyterians. There had, of course, been many smaller — even unsalubrious — chapels from 1780 onwards. These served enthusiastic but volatile congregations, given to rapid and frequent division. Several chapels, notably the Grape Lane chapel (demolished 1963), changed hands more than once: the incommodious Grape Lane building was used successively by Congregationalists, Lady Huntingdon's Connexion, the Methodist New Connexion, the Wesleyans, the Peculiar Baptists and the Primitive Methodists before it was eventually abandoned in 1851.

The 19th century was the heyday of chapel building — between 1800 and 1900 inclusive 20 places of worship were opened within the City walls; two of these were Roman Catholic churches (of which more later) two were Congregational chapels, one was Baptist, one Presbyterian and one Church of Christ. The rest were built, all 13 of them, by the various branches of the Methodist Church (Wesleyans, Primitive Methodists, United Methodist Free Church, New Connexion, etc.) Besides all this activity within the old City another 14 places of worship went up in the inner suburbs: these included a Salvation Army Citadel, another Roman Catholic church and — again — the rest were of the Methodist tradition.

The rapid proliferation of Nonconformist chapels is linked with the remarkable growth of the population of the City. In the fifth decade of the century the population increased by over 25% and, despite outbreaks of cholera and typhoid, numbers continued to increase, although not so rapidly, throughout the century and after.

Baptist meetings for worship began in 1862 at what came to be called the Victoria Hall in Goodramgate and two years later four people were actually baptised there. Two years later still (1866) the land in Priory Street was purchased on which the Baptist Church was built, and the church was finally opened in 1868.

As a railway centre and a garrison town York attracted an influx of Scots (as well as impoverished Irish Catholics) in the 19th century, with a Presbyterian background, and in 1879 the Presbyterian Church (now United Reformed Church) in Priory Street was built.

The 20th century has seen a decline in church and chapel attendance coupled with a tendency (only very recently halted) of people to remove from the walled city to the ever expanding suburbs and surrounding villages. This has had two effects — a number of chapels have closed or been sold to other bodies, and those that remain have either been remodelled and/or reduced in size, the galleries being of little use except on very special occasions. The Nonconformist tradition has not, it seems, clung to its buildings as the Anglican Church has and as chapels, with a few exceptions, date from the 19th or early 20th centuries, they have not until very recently acquired the status of historical buildings. Increasing interest in the architecture and furnishings of the last century may, in the future, perhaps, save chapels from demolition or unsuitable conversion if they fail to sustain congregations. Recent years have witnessed the destruction of important buildings such as Salem Chapel, St. Saviourgate and New Street Chapels, as well as the conversion to other uses of Lendal Chapel. Monk Bar Chapel and other smaller edifices. Change of use has not, however, always meant the secularisation of the building — Wesley Chapel in Priory Street has taken a new lease of life as the Assembly of God, just as the York Central Mission did in the 30s when the Pentecostals bought it, and as Victoria Bar Chapel is doing in the 90s.

The Roman Catholic population of York had a nunnery and boarding school for young ladies just *outside* the city walls, in Blossom Street in the late 17th century. Within the City a chapel was opened in Little Blake Street in 1760 which was replaced in 1802 by another larger chapel near the theatre. Nothing of these buildings survives but the coming of large numbers of Irish immigrants to the Walmgate area in the 1840s brought about the building of St. George's Church, to be followed a little later by St. Wilfrid's. Both were built in the Gothic style — unlike the Nonconformist chapels (with the exception of Priory Street Baptist Church) — and both were furnished in styles which reflected their continental models. St. Wilfrid's replaced the Chapel of 1802, and was for a short time — as St. George's had been earlier — the Roman Catholic pro-cathedral for the diocese of Beverley. This diocese was short lived; reorganisation divided the diocese between that of Leeds and Middlesbrough, the boundary being the River Ouse.

The most recent addition to Roman Catholic places of worship is the Shrine of St. Margaret Clitherow established in Shambles in c.1960 at what was at the time believed to be the house of the 16th-century martyr (1556-86).

WALK 1 — The South-west Area

Start: Rougier Street bus terminus
Finish: St. Michael's, Spurriergate Centre

This walk begins at a point where many visitors enter the city, especially those who have arrived by train or bus. The first church to be visited is one of the city's finest — **All Saints, North Street,** ① with its glorious introduction to the city's medieval stained glass. The walk ends at another notable church; this time converted to another use but still retaining a great number of interesting features — **St. Michael's, Spurriergate Centre.** ⑬ This building also can supply much needed refreshment which makes it a convenient terminus for those who embark on this church crawl.

From Rougier Street turn left into Tanner Row, and almost immediately right into All Saints Passage. This lane does a left turn after a short distance and **All Saints** ① appears. This church is usually open and is entered by the north door.

Leaving the church turn right and right again into North Street and continue past the Viking Hotel until the next road junction is reached, and — on the right — the former **St. John's Church,** ② now the Arts Centre. This is often open and has a small restaurant which may be useful especially if a late morning start has been made.

Here it is best to cross the road and turn right up Micklegate. After passing George Hudson Street on the right you find **St. Martin-cum-Gregory's** ③ Church on the left. If the church is open — perhaps for a sale of some kind — the entrance will be obvious (the north door). If not it is worth trying the south entrance via St. Martin's Lane. This will bring the visitor to the Mothers' Union Centre, and so to the church. Tea and coffee are available in the Centre.

The walk continues left up Micklegate hill, ignoring Trinity Lane on left to **Priory Church of the Holy Trinity,** ④ also on the left, just before a row of timber-framed buildings is reached. Holy Trinity is also usually open but may prove to be the last place of worship which can be entered — with the exception of St. Michael's — unless the walk is done on a Sunday when the still active churches and chapels are open for worship.

After leaving Holy Trinity turn left again and continue along Micklegate until Priory Street is reached. Here turn left for another view of Holy Trinity's west front (left) just before the **Assembly of God Chapel** ⑤ is reached. This was built as Wesley Chapel — note the ancillary buildings — and prior to the **Baptist Chapel** ⑥ opposite. Continue, still on the left hand side of Priory Street, to its end for a view of **St. Columba's United Reformed Church** ⑦ (originally Presbyterian). It is worth trying to imagine the scene in Priory Street before the removal of the tower of this church and that of the Baptist Chapel at the other end of this relatively new street.

At this point the visitor has to decide whether to continue along Lower Priory Street to Victor Street to see the outside of **Victoria Bar Chapel,** ⑧ and then down Victor Street, turning right into Cromwell Road to view the former **Church of Christ** ⑨ (now the Co-operative Society's Chapel of Rest), or to take a slightly

South-west Area

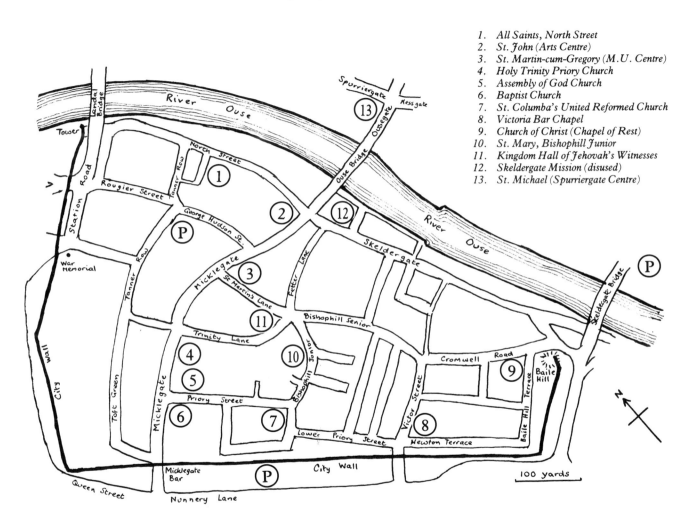

1. *All Saints, North Street*
2. *St. John (Arts Centre)*
3. *St. Martin-cum-Gregory (M.U. Centre)*
4. *Holy Trinity Priory Church*
5. *Assembly of God Church*
6. *Baptist Church*
7. *St. Columba's United Reformed Church*
8. *Victoria Bar Chapel*
9. *Church of Christ (Chapel of Rest)*
10. *St. Mary, Bishophill Junior*
11. *Kingdom Hall of Jehovah's Witnesses*
12. *Skeldergate Mission (disused)*
13. *St. Michael (Spurriergate Centre)*

shorter route to the end of the walk and refreshment.

If the shorter alternative is chosen turn left at the end of Priory Street into Bishophill Junior where the tower of **St. Mary's** ⑩ is immediately obvious just beyond a dancing school's premises. This church is usually locked but the noticeboard sometimes indicates where a key-holder can be located.

Continuing down Bishophill Junior you encounter a junction at which five roads meet. A very short distance down the first to the left is **Kingdom Hall of the Jehovah's Witnesses** ⑪ (on the right). A little further along on the left is the entrance to Jacob's Well, the parish room of Holy Trinity. If the longer alternative has been chosen the visitor, after viewing the Church of Christ in Cromwell Road, should retrace his steps along Cromwell Road and so into Bishophill Senior and thus to the five-road junction where the less energetic walker was left.

Both routes now combine and follow Fetter Lane which soon arrives in Skeldergate. Almost immediately opposite the end of Fetter Lane, to the right on the other side of Skeldergate, is all that remains of the once thriving **Skeldergate Mission,** ⑫ awaiting re-development. From here turn left until Micklegate is reached again and then turn right and so come to Ouse Bridge. Cross Ouse Bridge into Ousegate and so reach **St. Michael's Spurriergate Centre.** ⑬ If the right-hand side of the road over the bridge has been used, a good view of the clock at the west end of the church will tell the weary if they are in time for soup and sandwiches (or tea and cakes, as the case might be).

WALK 2 — The South-east Area

Start: South (or Marks & Spencer's) end of
        Shambles
Finish: High Ousegate — Parliament Street

Most visitors to York make a point of viewing Shambles, and **St. Crux Church Room** ① at the end of Shambles often provides light refreshments, especially on Saturdays and during the summer months, so this is a suitable starting point. The walk ends at **All Saints, Pavement,** ⑩ which is situated conveniently close to coffee shops, Jorvik Viking Centre and public toilets in the recently redesigned Parliament Street.

After a glimpse of **St. Crux,** ① should it be open, the walker sets off over the road down Fossgate. On the right look out for the entrance to the **Merchant Adventurers Hall** ② under a carved and painted heraldic panel. A small charge is made to view the Hall and Chapel, the outside of which will be seen later on this walk.

Leaving the Merchant Adventurers' Hall turn right, cross the pretty bridge over the Foss, and continue past the almshouses on the left into Walmgate.

For the time being ignore St. Denys Church and continue past the newspaper offices until the cast-iron gateway of **St. Margaret's** ③ appears on the left. This church is always locked but the south door is worth a visit. (Another Norman doorway is to be found at St. Lawrence's outside the city walls, which can be reached by extending the walk further along Walmgate, through Walmgate Bar and into Hull Road.)

From St. Margaret's cross Walmgate into Margaret Street and follow it until **St. George's Roman Catholic Church** ④ is reached at the junction with George Street. This church is open, but if a service is taking place cross the road to look at Dick Turpin's grave in the small churchyard opposite. Time could also be spent a short distance away to the north of the church in Chapel Row trying to imagine what **St. George's Methodist Chapel** ⑤ must have been like before it became a school and, now, a builder's store.

Continuing north-east along George Street, you reach Walmgate; turning left, retrace your steps to St. Denys Road (first on left) and another of the most interesting medieval parish churches of York — **St. Denys.** ⑥ The church is locked but a key is usually available locally (see noticeboard) and the search is well

South-east Area

1. St. Crux Church Room
2. Merchant Adventurers Chapel
3. St. Margaret (store)
4. St. George's Roman Catholic Church
5. St. George's Chapel (store)
6. St. Denys
7. Trinity Chapel (Fire Station)
8. Friends' Meeting House
9. St. Mary, Castlegate (The York Story)
10. All Saints', Pavement

14

worthwhile as the stained glass is remarkable, even by York standards.

Leaving St. Denys turn right along St. Denys Road into Piccadilly. There cross the road and turn right. After a couple of hundred yards the Foss is crossed and the route turns left along the Foss bank for a very short distance into the Castlegate car park. (Before leaving Piccadilly the outside of the **Merchant Adventurers Chapel** ② may be seen from the road, opposite Marks & Spencer's Food Store.)

Cross the car park to Tower Street and turn right into Clifford Street but notice the building at the left of the Fire Station opposite. It stands on the corner of Peckitt Street and the side in Peckitt Street reveals its Nonconformist chapel origins: **Trinity Chapel** ⑦. Continue along Clifford Street, passing the old frontage of the Friends Meeting House on the right, until it is possible to turn right into Friargate. Take this turning and half way along is the entrance to the **Friends Friargate Meeting House,** ⑧ which is often open.

At the top of Friargate turn right into Castlegate and then left to gain entrance to The York Story, in the former **St. Mary's, Castlegate** ⑨ There is a charge for admission and amongst other things a worthwhile audio-visual presentation which might provide a welcome rest.

Leaving The York Story, turn left into St. Mary's Square and so into Coppergate. Cross at the controlled pedestrian crossing, and with the tower of **All Saints'** ⑩ on the right, arrive in High Ousegate. Turn right here and so find the north door of the church which is usually open. After visiting this city centre church turn right and then left for Parliament Street (and the toilets), or left for Spurriergate — Coney Street (and refreshments and shops).

WALK 3 — The North-west Area

Start: St. Olave's, Marygate ①
Finish: Dean's Park, north of the Minster

This walk begins in the comparative calm of the Marygate area, where, despite the large car park, there is not much to detain the visitor to York, and leads through the busiest part of the city to another peaceful place, Dean's Park. In the summer months allow plenty of time to battle through the crowds and at all times beware the blandishments of the shops of Stonegate and Petergate: there is a good deal to see on this walk which finishes in the erudite surroundings of the Minster Library ⑬ (open week days) but within easy reach of restorative cafés such as those in the Treasurer's House (National Trust) and St. William's College. Toilet facilities are also available a short distance away at Bootham Bar.

Marygate is at right angles to Bootham, the principal entry to York from the north-west and the A19.

St. Olave's Church ① in a flowery churchyard stands close to the gatehouse of **St. Mary's Abbey.** ② After visiting the church which is open daily turn left towards the river and immediately left again into the grounds of the Yorkshire Museum. After a few yards the remains of the west wall of the great abbey church appear on the left beyond a rock garden. The substantial ruins, with the plan of the earlier Norman church marked on the lawn, stand beside the Yorkshire Museum and the walk takes the visitor past the entrance portico and so, beset by peacocks and squirrels, to the main entrance to the grounds in Museum Street. At this point look to the left for a good view of the west front of the Minster and St. Wilfrid's Church. Here cross with care into Lendal and from the corner near Peter Dominic's wine store view Lendal House, formerly **Lendal Congregational Chapel.** ③ Continue along Lendal passing the Judges' Lodging on the left and the Post Office on the right until the Mansion House (also on the right) is reached.

Here is St. Helen's Square which will be re-visited after a short excursion into Coney Street to see **St. Martin-le-Grand.** ④ The prominent clock and quiet memorial garden are always visible and the church is sometimes open for viewing.

15

North-west Area

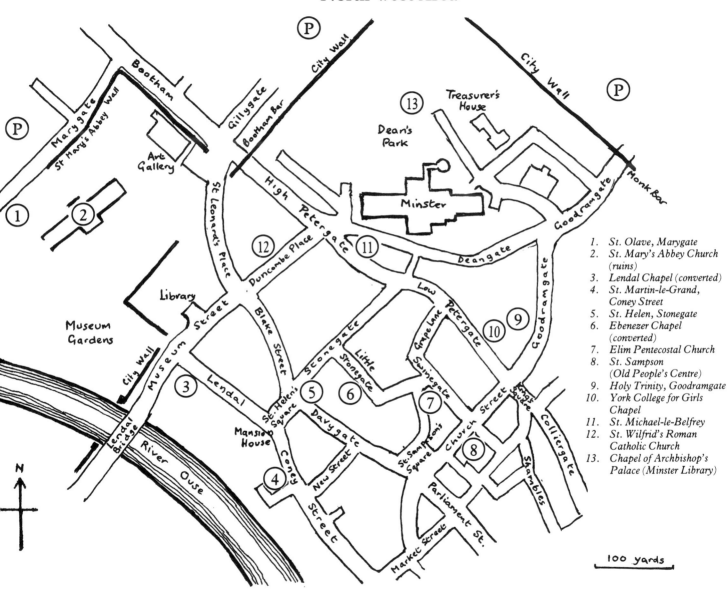

1. St. Olave, Marygate
2. St. Mary's Abbey Church (ruins)
3. Lendal Chapel (converted)
4. St. Martin-le-Grand, Coney Street
5. St. Helen, Stonegate
6. Ebenezer Chapel (converted)
7. Elim Pentecostal Church
8. St. Sampson (Old People's Centre)
9. Holy Trinity, Goodramgate
10. York College for Girls Chapel
11. St. Michael-le-Belfrey
12. St. Wilfrid's Roman Catholic Church
13. Chapel of Archbishop's Palace (Minster Library)

Return to St. Helen's Square and cross it for **St. Helen's Church**⑤ standing almost opposite Betty's famous café and between Crabtree and Evelyn's and the York Enterprise Centre. St. Helen's is open daily and is usually peaceful — buskers permitting.

Leaving St. Helen's turn right and right again into Stonegate and take the first turning on the right into Little Stonegate where, on the right again, is the former **Ebenezer Chapel**,⑥ now a printer's premises. The road bends to the left and becomes Back Swinegate, which is joined on the right by Finkle Street.

Between Finkle Street and Swinegate proper stands **Elim Pentecostal Church**,⑦ formerly the York Central Mission which can best be viewed from Swinegate. Turn right, therefore, into Swinegate, redeveloped attractively in 1991, and continue walking to Church Street, turning right and crossing the road for **St. Sampson's**⑧ **Old People's Centre,** which serves tea, coffee and light refreshments, Tuesdays to Saturdays. Retracing the walk in Church Street continue north- east with King's Square on the right, into Goodramgate looking carefully for the gateway to Holy Trinity Churchyard on the left, just before Lady Row — a range of early jettied buildings.

Holy Trinity, Goodramgate⑨ is redundant but usually open and appears very much as it must have done 250 years ago. From the base of the tower the back of the buildings in Low Petergate can be glimpsed. Some of these house **York College for Girls**⑩ whose **Chapel** on the first floor of a half-timbered building may be identified by its stained glass window. If Hornpot Lane is open (the gate is sometimes locked) the visitor may proceed straight into the crowds of Low Petergate and turn right past the imposing front of York College. If the lane is closed retrace the route in Goodramgate to King's Square and turn right, continuing along Low Petergate past Grape Lane (the site of another Nonconformist chapel, now demolished) and Stonegate — Minster Gates to High Petergate.

On the right, opposite the alleged birthplace of Guy Fawkes (whose parents' home was probably in Stonegate!) is **St. Michael-le-Belfrey**,⑪ close to the south-west tower of York Minster. St. Michael's is often open, especially in the summer months and should be visited if at all possible.

From St. Michael's the Roman Catholic Church of **St. Wilfrid**⑫ can be easily reached in Duncombe Place, to the left of the Dean Court Hotel. St. Wilfrid's is always open. From St. Wilfrid's the walk returns to the windy space outside the west front of the Minster and through the fine gates into Dean's Park where the **former Chapel of the Archbishop's Palace**⑬ (which no longer survives) may be seen in the north east-corner. The Minster Library is now housed in this building and its extensions; it is open to the public, Mondays to Fridays. More iron gates at the east end of the Library lead to a cobbled road, the Treasurer's House (National Trust) where there is a tea room and College Street which gives access to St. William's College, a Minster gift shop and exhibition and an excellent restaurant, opposite College Green where there are seats for the foot-sore.

WALK 4 — The North-east Area

Start: Outside the National Trust Shop at the
and junction of College Street and
Finish: Goodramgate

This circular walk begins (and ends) not far from the east end of York Minster. Here there are ample opportunities for refreshment and rest — notably St. William's College restaurant, the National Trust teashop and several picturesque and varied hostelries. Toilet facilities for those not patrons of the tea shops are available beyond Monk Bar, between Lord Mayor's Walk and the large car park.

Cross Goodramgate from the National Trust's shop and enter Bedern, where the remains of the **Chapel of**

North-east Area

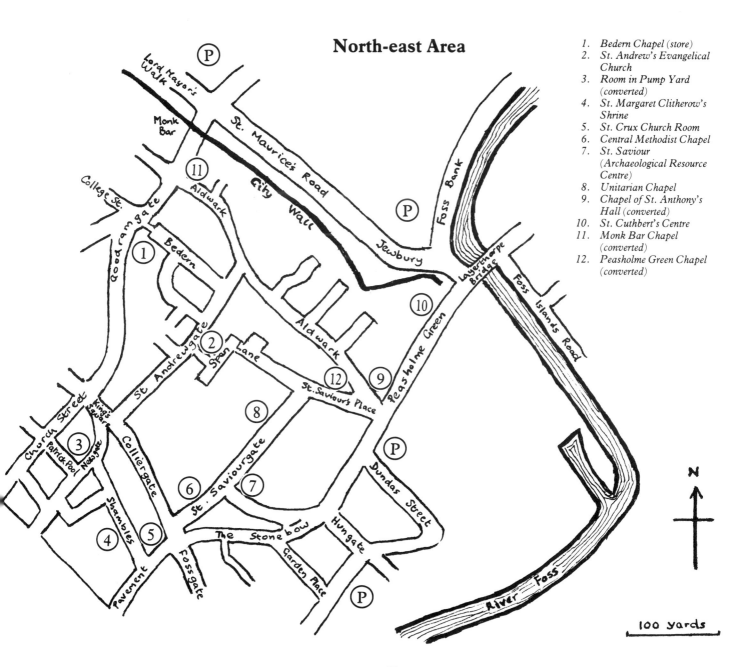

1. Bedern Chapel *(store)*
2. St. Andrew's Evangelical Church
3. Room in Pump Yard *(converted)*
4. St. Margaret Clitherow's Shrine
5. St. Crux Church Room
6. Central Methodist Chapel
7. St. Saviour *(Archaeological Resource Centre)*
8. Unitarian Chapel
9. Chapel of St. Anthony's Hall *(converted)*
10. St. Cuthbert's Centre
11. Monk Bar Chapel *(converted)*
12. Peasholme Green Chapel *(converted)*

100 yards

the **Vicars Choral**[1] of York Minster is located on the right. This is not open to the public. (The Vicars Choral in their day had a bridge over Goodramgate, perhaps in the vain hope that it would keep the Minster's singers unspotted from the world; one end of it may survive in the projection above a doorway of the National Trust premises.) Continue walking through the Bedern until St. Andrewgate is reached. Here turn right for **St. Andrew's**[2] Church, which is not usually open.

The walk continues along St. Andrewgate until King's Square is reached. Avoiding the remains of take-away food and jugglers, fire-eaters and crowds making for Shambles, cross the square into Newgate where on the right, at the junction with Patrick Pool, is an inscription recording **'the room in Pump Yard'**[3] in which John Wesley preached. Return a few yards and turn right into Shambles and walk in a south-easterly direction, keeping a sharp look out for the Shrine of **St. Margaret Clitherow**[4] on the right. This small dark heavily-restored room is usually open.

Continue to the end of Shambles where on the left is **St. Crux Church Room**,[5] sometimes open for charitable sales and often on summer Saturdays selling tea, coffee and light refreshments. Here turn left into Pavement and left again very briefly into Whipmawhopmagate before crossing Colliergate into St. Saviourgate. On the left the powerful frontage of the **Central Methodist Chapel**[6] (formerly Centenary Chapel) confronts the concrete nastiness of Stonebow House. The chapel is in frequent use and is worth a visit. Continuing along St. Saviourgate **St. Saviour's Church**,[7] now the Archaeological Resource Centre (A.R.C.), is reached; this is open to visitors as a rule for a modest fee.

The walk continues past Lady Hewley's Almshouses on the right to the **Unitarian Chapel**,[8] on the left behind excellent cast-iron railings.

At the end of St. Saviourgate turn right into St. Saviour's Place (Hilary House replaces the demolished Salem Chapel, alas) and so reach Peasholme Green. On the left, at the corner of Aldwark, is **St. Anthony's Hall**,[9] now the University of York's Borthwick Institute, which used to have a **chapel** at ground floor level. The blocked 'south' doorway and 'east' window can be easily picked out before continuing along Peasholme Green towards Layerthorpe Bridge. On the right a large area awaits redevelopment and on the left is **St. Cuthbert's Church**,[10] just within the City wall. St. Cuthbert's, now the Administrative Centre for St. Michael-le-Belfrey, is usually open to visitors.

At this point two alternatives present themselves: the first involves a walk along the City wall from Layerthorpe Bridge to Monk Bar, but this misses the oldest Methodist Chapel at Peasholme Green (although it is actually at the south-eastern end of Aldwark, behind Hilary House). If this route is taken descend from the Wall at Monk Bar, as you must, cross the road but do not continue along the wall. Instead turn left and notice the frontage of the turf accountant's premises on the left as you walk towards the city centre.

This large building which can also be viewed from Aldwark is the former **Monk Bar Chapel**.[11] A few more yards along Goodramgate and the walk is over.

The second alternative involves retracing the route from St. Cuthbert's to Aldwark, where you turn right past St. Anthony's Hall chapel and almost immediately on the left a large brick building, now a dental surgery, is the earliest surviving Methodist chapel in York — **Peasholme Green Chapel**.[12] Like the other converted buildings it is not open to the public — unless the visitor is suddenly stricken with dental decay, a situation not to be contemplated.

Passing Peasholme Green Chapel then, proceed along Aldwark, admiring the delectable modern housing and the Hall of the Merchant Taylors on the right, well off the road, until the rear of the buildings in Goodramgate is visible across a yard on the right. Here is the back of the former **Monk Bar Chapel**.[11] At the road junction cross the road and glance back at the (changed) front of Monk Bar Chapel before turning towards the City centre. A few yards along Goodramgate the entry to Bedern is seen on the left and the walk is accomplished.

St. Wilfred's Church, Duncombe Place.

St. Saviour's Church:
now the Archaeological Resource Centre.

Alphabetical list of Churches and Chapels

The former ABBEY CHURCH of ST. MARY

Between the City walls and St. Olave's Church in Marygate stand the impressive remains of St. Mary's Abbey Church founded for Benedictine monks in 1088 by William Rufus.

The ruins are mainly those of the north and west walls of the Abbey Church of the late 13th Century. The Abbey was suppressed in 1539 and the buildings became a quarry, stone being taken for the repair of, for example, St. Olave's nearby.

St. Mary: The Blessed Virgin Mary, mother of Jesus Christ, the most venerated of all the Saints and the most popular in medieval England.

St. Mary's Abbey:
North nave wall.

ALL SAINTS, North Street

The approach to All Saints Church is by way of a rather unpromising passage which leaves Tanner Row between a public house and a betting shop, near the bus terminus in Rougier Street. Alternatively the church can be reached from North Street (dominated by the Viking Hotel), and All Saints Lane alongside some charming timber-framed cottages.

The earliest reference to a church here is dated 1089 but the building is said to incorporate re-used Roman stone. The 15th-century tower and spire are thin and elegant and close by is an early 20th-century 'anchorage' designed by Ridsdale Tate, who also designed the chancel screens in 1906.

All Saints, North Street:
The spire from the south-west.

All Saints, North Street:
Rubbing of part of the brass to Thomas Atkinson, now removed.

This latter window may be the work of John Thornton of Coventry who made the great east window of the Minster. The east window of the north aisle is 14th-century with a charming nativity scene, and the early 15th-century east window of the main aisle shows two donors both called Nicholas Blackburn, merchants and Lord Mayors, with their wives — both of them

All Saints, North Street:
Visiting the prisoners, from the Acts of Mercy window.

Restoration of the church after 1975 cleared away much holy clutter assembled during the long incumbency of the greatly beloved Father Shaw (1904-1950) which had given the church the most convincing medieval atmosphere of all York churches. Now the church remains notable for a pulpit of 1675, a memorial to architect William Etty who died in 1708, a fine medieval roof and — above all — glorious 14th and 15th-century glass.

Windows in the north aisle show the Six Corporal Acts of Mercy and the Last Fifteen Days of the World (the 'Pricke of Conscience' window, based on a poem by Richard Rolle of Hampole, a Yorkshire mystic).

All Saints, North Street:
Guardian angel bearing a soul.

Margarets — kneeling below a tender St. Anne teaching the Virgin Mary to read, flanked by St. Christopher and St. John Baptist.

ALL SAINTS, Pavement

All Saints, Pavement, stands at the junction of High Ousegate and Coppergate, overlooking but not now actually in Pavement. Its striking octagonal lantern tower was originally built between 1475-1501 and a lamp was kept burning at night, it is said, to guide people approaching York from the north through the Forest of Galtres. Today the light burns as a memorial to the dead of two world wars.

The church is mentioned in the Domesday survey, but the present building lost its chancel in 1782 and other parts more recently. It was extensively restored in the 1830s and 1880s.

The way into the church is the north door in High Ousegate: it has a splendid door ring, probably 13th-century, depicting a lion swallowing a bearded head. Within all is well-cared for as befits an important Gild church in the City centre. Notable furnishings include a 1634 pulpit by Nicholas Hall, mayoral boards and royal arms, and a 15th-century lectern (from the demolished church of St. Crux) with carved evangelists on the stem. The late 14th-century glass in the west

Octagonal lantern tower of All Saints, Pavement.

All Saints, Pavement:
Door plate and ring, north door.

November 1st is All Saints' Day. More churches in England have this dedication than any other, with the exception of St. Mary, the Blessed Virgin.

Tate Wilkinson (1739-1803)

Tate Wilkinson was the son of a clergyman and the contemporary of Garrick and Sheridan. As an actor he appeared at Covent Garden and elsewhere, his parts including young women's. It is hard to judge of his success as an actor but as a mimic he was unrivalled. His impressions of other actors were usually taken in good part but he is said to have offended Garrick.

He invested £1,400 in theatrical ventures in Yorkshire and Newcastle — a considerable sum in those days — and appeared as Coriolanus in York in 1766. He became the patentee of the York theatre in 1769 and was in sole charge of theatres in York, Hull

Tate Wilkinson, buried in All Saints, Pavement.
(York Minster Library).

window came from redundant St. Saviour's at the other end of Pavement, and there are four good windows by Kempe.

Monuments include one to Tate Wilkinson, licensee of the Theatre Royal, who died in 1803, and another to Mr. Henry Richards, who died in 1783 after nearly 60 years' soldiering at such battles as Dettingen, Fountenoy and Culloden: he must have begun his military career at a very tender age as he was only 68 at his death.

All Saints is one of the most popular of dedications, and commemorates all those saints who are not otherwise remembered on a special day in the Church's calendar.

and Newcastle in 1770. He later managed theatres in Leeds and Edinburgh also.

In his time as actor-manager the Yorkshire theatres rivalled those of Bath and he engaged the distinguished and notorious (from 'Mrs. Siddons to dancing dogs' as the Dictionary of National Biography puts it). From 1778 he styled himself 'the Wandering Patentee' and despite everything he made money. He was popular, a *bon viveur*, a wit and a free liver behind whose gruff manner lay a kindly disposition.

He married in York and he and his wife are commemorated in All Saints, Pavement.

ST. ANDREW

St. Andrew's Church stands at the junction of St. Andrewgate and Spen Lane amidst attractive recent redevelopment of a formerly run-down area of York, to the east of Goodramgate.

St. Andrew's Evangelical Church from the west.

A simple building, St. Andrew's lacks aisles and tower and has had a chequered history. In 1547 an Act of Parliament gave the Corporation of York the opportunity to reduce the number of its churches from about 40 to 25. Many were demolished for their stone and lead and in 1559 St. Andrew's was closed. By 1576 the parson of St. Saviour's was criticised for keeping his 'swyne' in St. Andrew's churchyard, and later still the building was used variously as a stable, a brothel and St. Peter's School, presumably not simultaneously. By 1924 it was called 'The Gospel Hall' and used by the 'open' Plymouth Brethren. The building has now reverted to its proper function and is used by a vigorous evangelical congregation of about 100.

A Perpendicular window remains, and also the 15th-century timber roof. There is a recently unblocked chancel arch and the framework of a former bell turret. Restoration has taken place during 1991 at a cost of £60,000 to give increased space by the opening up of the former chancel which was until recently a tiny dwelling.

St. Andrew: was one of the Twelve Apostles and the brother of Simon Peter. Originally a fisherman, he is now the patron saint of Scotland.

ASSEMBLY OF GOD (formerly WESLEY CHAPEL), Priory Street

Priory Street occupies the site of the grounds of Holy Trinity Priory and proved attractive to Nonconformists in the last century; the Methodists, Baptists and Presbyterians all built places of worship here.

Approaching from Micklegate the visitor will find the Assembly of God Church on the left — a substantial red-brick and stone building with fine railings. Until 1983 this was known as Wesley Chapel and served a Methodist congregation.

The building, dating from 1856, was designed by James Simpson of Leeds, the architect of the Central

Methodist (formerly Centenary) Chapel in St. Saviourgate. Here he provided the Methodists with what is now the second largest auditorium in the City (after York Minster), seating 1,200 people, also a school, a house for the headmaster, and a caretaker's house.

The Assembly of God congregation took over the chapel in March, 1983, renovating and redecorating the handsome interior very successfully. The pine pews in the gallery and the oak pews in the body of the church remain unchanged as does the pulpit and organ. Early 20th-century glass fills the lower windows; the upper have almost *art nouveau* motifs.

The pulpit has been used by numerous notable speakers including Dr. Billy Graham, the missionary Gladys Aylward, Pastor Martin Niemöller and Sir Stafford Cripps.

The former BEDERN CHAPEL

All that remains of the Chapel of the Vicars Choral of York Minster may be seen on the right-hand side of Bedern as it is entered from Goodramgate, almost opposite College Street.

The Chapel was consecrated in 1349 and, after being ruinous for many years, has been partially restored. It

Wesley Chapel (now Assembly of God) by James Simpson.

Interior of Wesley Chapel from the gallery.

Restored remnant of the Bedern Chapel.

was dedicated to the Holy Trinity, the Virgin Mary and Saint Katharine. By the 1830s when it was described as 'still entire' the building was being used as a Sunday School.

Now the Chapel is used as a store by York Minster's works department.

Bedern: Anglo-Saxon for 'house of prayer'.

Holy Trinity: see under Holy Trinity, Goodramgate.

The Virgin Mary: see under St. Mary, Bishophill Junior.

St. Katharine: or Catherine of Alexandria, supposedly 4th-century but probably mythical. Her legend tells that she refused marriage with the emperor, disputed successfully with pagan philosophers and was finally beheaded after torture on a wheel which broke, injuring by-standers (hence the firework of the name).

Amongst others she was regarded as the patron of young girls, students (and hence the clergy), nurses and wheelwrights, millers and so forth.

In England 62 ancient churches were dedicated in her name.

CENTRAL METHODIST (formerly CENTENARY) CHAPEL, St. Saviourgate

St. Saviourgate runs north-east from the point at which Colliergate meets Pavement. Like Priory Street this street housed several Nonconformist chapels, but now is over-shadowed by the notorious Stonebow House with its intrusive dirty concrete and mis-placed car park.

The mighty facade of what to generations of York Methodists has always been 'Centenary Chapel' (with the stress of the *first* syllable of Centenary) still contrives to dominate St. Saviourgate, and was the work of James Simpson of Leeds in 1839-40. (Later he was commissioned to produce a very different but equally dignified chapel for the Wesleyans in Priory Street.) The imposing Ionic pillars of the portico, like

other parts of the stirrup-shaped chapel, have subsided and require very expensive and extensive remedial treatment.

Designed to seat 1,500 people, the interior, full of box pews under a coffered ceiling decorated with acanthus leaf bosses will even now, after some modification, accommodate over 1,000.

The two-decker Spanish mahogany pulpit has been

James Simpson's Centenary Chapel (now Central Methodist Church).

Interior of Centenary Chapel, St. Saviourgate.

of York, stands at the point at which Aldwark meets Peasholme Green.

This hall originally belonged to the Gild of St. Martin but seems always to have been called St. Anthony's. The oldest buildings here date from 1446-53 and included a chapel of which only a blocked doorway with niches and an altered east window survive.

In 1593 the chapel was still in use, a bell being rung for half an hour to summon worshippers at 7am and 4.45pm in winter and 6am and 6pm in summer.

reduced and lowered, but the original ruby, orange and blue flashed glass windows remain.

Centenary: refers to the centenary of Methodism. This chapel was built as a 'cathedral of Methodism' at that anniversary.

The former CHAPEL OF ST. ANTHONY'S HALL

St. Anthony's Hall, now housing the Borthwick Institute of Historical Research, part of the University

The former CHAPEL OF THE ARCHBISHOP'S PALACE

The former Chapel of the Archbishop's Palace is situated in Dean's Park to the north of the Minster. The palace itself ceased to be used by the Archbishops

*Remains of the chapel of St. Anthony's Hall:
altered 'east' window on right.*

*Reconstructed Chapel of the Archbishop's Palace,
now the Minster Library.*

Impression of the upper Chapel prior to restoration.
(York Minster Library).

of York in the mid-16th century and all that remained was finally demolished in the early 19th century.

The Chapel was built by Walter de Grey about 1230 making it contemporary with the south transept of the Minster, and restored substantially 1806-11 to serve as the Minster Library. It is a plain rectangular building of two storeys, housing the largest cathedral library in England.

THE CHAPEL OF THE MERCHANT ADVENTURERS

The impressive Great Hall of the Company of Merchant Adventurers of the City of York stands back in its attractive garden from busy Piccadilly but is approached under a splendid armorial panel at 40 Fossgate, a short distance from Foss Bridge.

A religious, charitable and fraternal gild dedicated to Our Lord and the Blessed Virgin Mary built a chapel and other premises in Fossgate in the second half of the 14th century. The gild was short-lived and by the 1420s the Mercers had taken over. A chapel, attached to the

undercroft, was licensed in 1411, and in 1581 the Mercers Gild became the Company of the Merchant Adventurers.

The undercroft was used as a 'hospital' (or almshouse) originally for old ladies, but latterly for five old ladies and five old men. Despite the raising of the floor level both Hospital and Chapel were — and are — liable to flooding, so perhaps the old people needed to

The badge of the Hospital of 'The Blessed Virgin Mary next to Foss Bridge, York'.

be fairly sprightly if they were to enjoy the charity of the Gild. In 1982 water rose half way up the Communion rail.

The Chapel — now the Trinity Chapel — is furnished in mid 17th-century style and has recently been repainted in the original colours of the 1660s. Boards record that the chapel was repaired and beautified in 1756, 1801, 1820, 1846, and it was more

The east window is filled with blue and white glass.

recently refurbished in memory of Noel Goddard Terry who was Governor of the Merchant Adventurers 1935-7.

THE CHAPEL OF YORK COLLEGE FOR GIRLS

At 62 Low Petergate is the attractive Georgian entrance to York College for Girls whose premises extend behind the neighbouring shops. Behind 64 Low Petergate is a surprise: the 20th-century columns support a house which appears to be of 18th-century date — the rainwater head is dated 1763 — but this is a mere front to a timber-framed building originating in the 15th century. It is in this building, on the first floor, that the College Chapel is situated. The Chapel was dedicated by Archbishop Ramsey in 1960. The altar cross and candlesticks are in memory of the first two

Chapel of the Merchant Adventurers seen through the 15th-century screen.

The rear of 64 Low Petergate:
The Chapel of York College is on the first floor.

The sanctuary of the Chapel of York College for Girls.

headmistresses of the College, Elizabeth E. Ellett, 1908-1935, and Frances I. Savory, 1935-1943. The small and very attractive stained glass window of 1960 is by Harry Stammers 'in memory of Herbert and Bertha Swift to whose faith and vision the foundation of York College in 1908 was largely due'. One of the shepherds in the window is a likeness of Eric Milner-White, Dean of York, 1941-1963.

The Very Revd. Eric Milner-White (1884-1963)

Eric Milner-White was educated at Harrow and King's College, Cambridge where he was later Fellow, Chaplain and finally, Dean. Devout, a liturgist and connoisseur of beautiful things, he was a man of many interests as varied as pottery, the ballet and the engineering earthworks of the North Eastern Railway.

He came to York as Dean in 1941, bringing his knowledge of stained glass, acquired at King's College, Cambridge, and put to good use restoring and re-ordering the Minster's glass after the Second World War. The author of several volumes of prayers, he introduced the now world-famous Festival of Nine Lessons and Carols on Christmas Eve, first to King's and later to York Minster. He also devised an Epiphany Procession service and took a strong interest in the performance of these and the routine services. He served happily on the literary panel which translated the New English Bible, and also — less happily, as might be expected — on the Liturgical Commission. Dean Milner-White played an important part in founding York's Civic Trust; he left his pottery collection to York Art Gallery, and the University of York partly owes its existence to his enthusiasm for

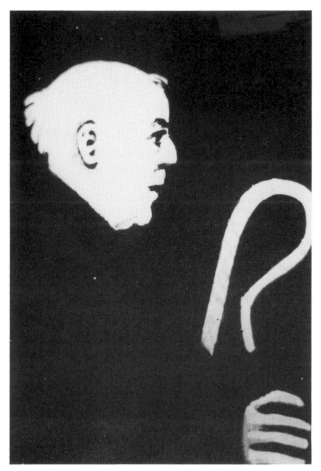

Stained glass window detail showing
The Very Revd. Eric Milner-White as a shepherd.

The former CHURCH OF CHRIST CHAPEL, Cromwell Road

Not far from Baile Hill in Cromwell Road stands a red brick chapel with a Dutch-style gable, echoing the now demolished warehouse in nearby Skeldergate. This was built after the demolition of the House of Correction which stood on this site until 1880, having been closed over ten years previously.

North Yorkshire Co-operative Society's Chapel of Rest:
Formerly Church of Christ Chapel.

education. He was chairman of the governors of St. Peter's School and Provost of the Northern Division of Woodard Schools, of which York College for Girls is one.

He died in 1963 and his ashes and memorial are at the foot of the great crucifix in the Minster's south transept.

The Chapel dates from 1889. Until 1905 it belonged to the Church (or Disciples) of Christ.

In later years Free Church Pentecostals had the use of the building from 1953.

Later still it became a wholesale chemist's warehouse and in 1959 a Cooperative Society's Funeral Service Chapel of Rest.

ST. COLUMBA, Priory Street

On the west side of Priory Street, at its junction with Bishophill Junior, stands the United Reformed Church of St. Columba, built for the Presbyterians in 1879 to designs by T. B. Thompson of Hull. A white brick building, it appears at its best from the corner of Bishophill Junior.

The tower (without the cupola of the original design, which was never built) of St. Columba's was removed in 1949, but fine cast-iron railings remain. Inside are the usual gallery (with most seats removed) and three stained glass windows, two bearing the badges of Scottish regiments — reminders that York was an important garrison town until recently.

Original design for St. Columba's. the cupola was never built.

St. Columba's:
The front interior was re-ordered in 1970.

T. B. Thompson's Presbyterian Chapel
without its tower.

St. Columba: founder of monasteries in Ireland and, most importantly, Iona in 563. Regarded as the Apostle of Scotland he retained his Irish connexions, as well as being a poet scholar and spiritual counsellor. He died in 597, in church before Matins. Buried on Iona, his remains were subsequently removed to Dunkeld in 849.

St. Columba:
Detail of memorial window to the Revd. James H. Collie (died 1912).

Engraving of 1813 (from H. Cave: Antiquities of York)*:*
St. Crux Church on right.

St. Crux Church Room incorporates details of the demolished church.

ST. CRUX

The tiny building situated at the Pavement end of Shambles and Whipmawhopmagate is obviously one with ecclesiastical connexions, but is in fact a church room on consecrated ground used for sales of work, jumble sales and coffee mornings for charitable purposes.

Monument to Sir Robert Watter and wife, erected between her death (1608) and his (1612).

This building replaced an ancient church, mentioned in Domesday Book, which was demolished in 1884-7. This church was the unmarked burial place of Thomas Percy, 7th Earl of Northumberland, who was beheaded in Pavement for his part in the Rising of the North.

The parish room of St. Crux contains splendidly restored monuments from the demolished church — an inscribed brass to Sir Thomas Herbert who was born over the road, a cheerfully coloured monument to Sir Robert Watter who died in 1612 and his wife who died in 1608, and an unflattering profile of Henry Waite (died 1780) by Fisher, as well as memorials to an apothecary, an ironmonger. a wine merchant, a hosier and linen draper, a haberdasher, rectors, a rear-admiral, an innkeeper, a surgical instrument-maker and a goldsmith (amongst others), many of whom were Lord Mayor or Sheriff in their day.

St. Crux: 'Saint' is from the Latin *sanctus* = holy. *Crux* = Cross, hence 'the Holy Cross'. Relics of the Cross on which Jesus Christ was put to death are said to have been discovered in Jerusalem in 326 by St. Helen, the mother of the first Christian Roman emperor Constantine. This is an appropriate dedication, perhaps, in view of York's link with Constantine.

ST. CUTHBERT, Peasholme Green

Just within the city walls at their north-eastern extremity stands the little church of St. Cuthbert. It is surrounded by a pleasant (but not easy to keep clear of rubbish) churchyard in a quarter of the city due for extensive re-development. An over-view of the church can be gained from the City wall as it descends to the Foss at Layerthorpe Bridge, and the church can be reached by braving the horrors of the Stonebow and continuing along Peasholme Green in the direction of the light industrial and commercial wastes of Layerthorpe-Foss Islands Road. The church is mentioned in Domesday Book and there is evidence of Saxon building on the site. It has been claimed that the church was actually founded in St. Cuthbert's time (7th century): this is improbable.

The church was saved from destruction in 1547 by Sir Martin Bowes, a former Lord Mayor of London, who gave York its Sword of State. He had lived at what is now the Black Swan public house in Peasholme Green.

The church's interior was remodelled about ten years ago to serve as the parish centre for St. Michael-le-Belfrey after the St. Cuthbert's congregation out-

St. Cuthbert from the south-east: note the exceptionally wide span of the roof.

grew the building in the time of the Revd. David Watson, and transferred to St. Michael's in 1973. The nave has been filled with a two-tier glass 'box', the upper floor approached by a staircase in the tower and a short 'bridge'. This box contains offices, a kitchen, consulting rooms and a reception area.

The church has a late 15th-century tower, a 500-

St. Cuthbert: modern window in the tower.

year-old door, a 17th-century pulpit (now without its base) and altar table of similar date. A cartouche memorial to Charles Mitley, carver, who died in 1758 survives, and a modern window in the tower depicts St. Cuthbert holding the head of King Oswald.

The mother of General Wolfe, Henrietta Thompson, lived as a child at the Black Swan and no doubt worshipped at St. Cuthbert's, so the church has a special interest for Canadian visitors.

St. Cuthbert: a monk and, later, bishop of Lindisfarne (or Holy Island) 685-687. He had connexions with Melrose, Ripon and Hexham and was a much-loved spiritual leader. Although he was buried on Lindisfarne, his remains, said to be incorrupt, were removed after Danish raids, and eventually came to rest in Durham Cathedral. His coffin, portable altar, pectoral cross and fragments of vestments can still be seen at Durham. There is a notable 15th-century window commemorating him in the south-east transept of York Minster. This shows him carrying the head of King and Saint Oswald (as in St. Cuthbert's modern window) which was buried with St. Cuthbert's remains.

ST. DENYS, Walmgate

The church of St. Denys stands in its raised churchyard, as on an island, at the junction of St. Denys Road and Walmgate. The churchyard is bounded on the other two sides by unprepossessing lanes, one flanking an overpowering office block, the other confusingly called Dennis Street. The church-yard is attractive and the interior was described by an unknown passer-by as 'the best-kept church in York'.

The earliest reference to St. Denys' Church is in the third quarter of the 12th century, but the present church is mainly from the 13th and 14th centuries, much modified and rebuilt. The fine Norman doorway (one of three in this part of York) is not *in situ*, and the tower, rebuilt in 1847, was originally at the crossing. This used to be the Fishmongers' Church, but also

St. Denys, with re-sited Norman doorway.

St. Denys: border and quarries from north aisle window (14th-century).

contained the burial vault of the Earls of Northumberland who had a residence called Percy's Inn in Walmgate. The vault has not been located but is said to contain the remains of the 3rd Earl who died after the Battle of Towton, Palm Sunday, 1461, leading the Lancastrian army.

The great glory of the church is its wealth of 14th and 15th-century stained glass. The three great east windows are imposing in a church which is wider than it is long, and the early-13th-century roundels on grisaille backgrounds are the oldest glass in York parish churches. The east window of the north aisle is the best feature, and there is a 14th-century Jesse window in the north aisle.

Interesting monuments include one to Dorothy Wilson who died in 1717 (she endowed the hospital or almshouse near Foss Bridge in Walmgate, opposite Stubbs the Ironmongers) and another to Mr. Hotham who died in 1806. The latter is by a member of the Fisher family of York sculptors.

St. Denys: was a bishop of Paris who died about 250. He is the patron saint of France, having been sent from Italy as a missionary to Gaul. Over 40 ancient churches in England were dedicated to St. Denys (who is also known as Dennis and Dionysius). It is strange that the parish named after the patron saint of France should adjoin the parish of St. George, patron of England.

The former EBENEZER CHAPEL, Little Stonegate

On the south-west side of Little Stonegate, which leads from Stonegate to Swinegate, are the rather grim remains of Ebenezer Chapel, opened on 13 November, 1851. Designed by York architect J. P. Pritchett for the Primitive Methodists who had previously worshipped at the (now-demolished) chapel in Grape Lane, a mere 75 yards away, the building served as a place of worship for half a century before being sold to a firm of printers in 1901.

The chapel had two galleries, and some of the interior woodwork survives amongst the printing machinery.

Ebenezer: 'a stone of help'. 1 Samuel 7 v. 12 records that a stone memorial called 'Stone of help' was erected to mark the end of the Philistine war in the time of Samuel. The name Ebenezer was popular for Baptist and Methodist chapels.

ELIM PENTECOSTAL CHURCH (formerly THE YORK CENTRAL MISSION), Swinegate

On a corner site between Swinegate and Finkle Street, with its frontage onto Swinegate stands Elim Pentecostal Church. These premises were built for a non-sectarian mission, led in the beginning by two Methodists, and opened on 27 June, 1910. The building of red and purplish-grey brick includes the hall to seat 800 people, a lecture room, school rooms and offices. Bands of red brick with incised initials facing Back Swinegate and numerous foundation stones suggest that many contributed to this venture.

In 1915 the building was requisitioned for what the Victoria County History enigmatically calls 'war

J. P. Pritchett's Ebenezer Chapel, Little Stonegate, is now a printing works.

Initials of contributors to the York Central Mission, now Elim Pentecostal Church.

Front entrance to Elim Pentecostal Church.

of the city. Bare rafters, tip-up seats (surely ex-cinema) and blue-curtained apse are all functional rather than attractive.

Elim: a place visited by the Hebrews on their escape from Egypt under Moses. Exodus 15 v.27 and 16 v.1: 'And they came to Elim, where were twelve walls of water, and threescore and ten palm trees: and they encamped there by the waters. And they took their journey from Elim...' (A.V.)

FRIENDS MEETING HOUSE, Friargate

The stretch of Friargate between Clifford Street and Castlegate gives access to the Friends Meeting House. Quakers have worshipped on this site since 1674 and Minute Books dating back to 1670 are now housed in the Brotherton Library, Leeds University. The modern building, opened in March, 1981, replaces older premises built originally in 1718 and rebuilt 100 years later. These included a Large Meeting House which seated over 1,000 people.

In the 1914-18 war this sheltered Belgian refugees and was later used for a hospital. Pupils from Bootham

The 1981 remodelled Meeting House entrance. The columns came from the demolished large Meeting House.

purposes'; perhaps the later use of part of the building as a snooker hall began at this time. The mission closed in 1934 and opened for worship by Elim Pentecostal Church in 1935.

The interior of the church itself is typical of Nonconformist chapels but lacks the elegance and impressiveness of the Methodist and Baptist Churches

School (founded in 1823) and The Mount School (founded 1831) as well as patients and staff from 'The Retreat' (the Quaker mental hospital) all worshipped here until meetings in their own premises became more practical. This Large Meeting House became unsafe — it was not used after 1978 — and was finally demolished and the Clifford Street frontage sold. However, the Small Meeting House of 1884 which seats about 200 people has been retained in the present building and the facade incorporates a number of cast-iron columns which supported the gallery in the Large Meeting House; these add simple dignity to the building and help it blend with the somewhat Dickensian surroundings of solicitors, stationers and church in Castlegate.

The premises include a library, offices, a warden's house and — in the basement — a Records Room and the Peace Centre.

The architect for the new Meeting House was Denis Mason Jones of Leeds.

ST. GEORGE, George Street

St. George's is situated at the junction of George Street and Margaret Street on the edge of post-war housing development which replaced the slums behind Walmgate. Its rather dour and daunting exterior, not helped by cement rendering in places, entirely belies its warm, friendly and welcoming interior. The church was built between 1847 and 1849 for the Roman Catholic Irish immigrant population which had settled in this part of York. The design was by J. A. and C. Hansom who lived in Micklegate. (J. A. Hansom was also the designer of the Hansom Cab and had been keen to be

Commemorative tablets in the entrance to the Meeting House.

St. George's Roman Catholic Church and Presbytery.

40

Memorial in the churchyard of the now vanished medieval church of St. George of the Beanhills.

the architect when St. Wilfrid's was planned.) St. George's was restored and modified in 1990 but only eventually consecrated in the spring of 1991.

The east window contains glass by Hardman, possibly designed by Pugin. The Bartholomew's Guide to York describes the Barnett glass in the side chapel as being 'the colours of jellies' — appropriate enough in a city of confectioners. The churchyard, over the road, is

J. A. Hansom's other achievement is commemorated by the public house in Market Street.

The Bishop of Middlesbrough at the consecration of St. George's, 1991.

that of an earlier medieval St. George's Church (St. George of the Beanhills) demolished long ago. It is notable for the tombstone of Richard Palmer (or Turpin) executed at Tyburn on the Knavesmire, April 7, 1739 'notorious highwayman and horse stealer'. It is also the burial place of the victims of the Asiatic cholera outbreak in 1832.

When Roman Catholic bishops were re-established in England in 1851 St. George's became for 14 years the cathedral of the diocese of Beverley.

St. George: was martyred about 303 at Lydda during the persecution of Diocletian. He was probably a Roman soldier. The legend of the slaughter of the dragon is, sadly, late and doubtful. St. George has been known in England since the 7th or 8th century and Richard I and the Crusaders adopted him, thus preparing the way for his patronage of England. His cult was downgraded in 1969 but over 160 ancient (and more modern) churches are dedicated to this patron of soldiers, knights, archers and armourers, who was invoked by sufferers from plague, leprosy and (significantly?) syphilis. St. George, of course, is often represented with his dragon and the red cross on the white background.

The former ST. GEORGE'S CHAPEL, Walmgate

At the end of Chapel Row, between George Street and Walmgate is a disused Methodist Chapel built in three months in 1826.

The Wesleyan Methodist congregation here declined when Centenary Methodist Chapel opened in 1840, but the building survived as a mission chapel and school. In 1845 the day school at St. George's started. This was not accepted by the School Board in 1870 and in 1897 became a Roman Catholic school. This closed in 1978 and at present the building is used as a builder's store. The conversion from chapel to school has left little to indicate the original function of the building.

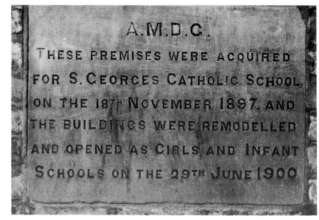

'To the Greater Glory of God'. Tablet on north-west wall of the former St. George's Chapel.

ST. HELEN

St. Helen's Church stands across the square of the same name from the Mansion House at the corner of Stonegate and Davygate. St. Helen's Square was created after the sale of the churchyard to the City in

St. Helen's Church in 1838. (From an engraving in Hargrove's New Guide.)

St. Helen's, Stonegate — but actually in St. Helen's Square.

glass painters lived and worked in Stonegate — and the west window of the south aisle has a roundel with their arms. The matching window of the north aisle shows a Blue Coat boy.★

The font is an odd affair — a late 12th-century bowl sits on an inverted 15th-century capital on a 13th-century base. Another odd contraption was set up against the tower of St. Helen's in 1603 when James I was visiting the City; it evidently produced a fountain of wine — no doubt for a very limited period.

A monument in the south aisle (east end) commemorates two spinster sisters who both lived for 98 years, spanning seven reigns. Barbara (1667-1765)

NEAR THIS PLACE LIE THE BODIES OF
TWO MAIDEN SISTERS,
BARBARA AND ELIZABETH DAVYES,
EACH HAVING COMPLETED HER 98ᵗʰ YEAR,
BARBARA WAS BORN IN 1667 AND DIED IN 1765,
ELIZABETH WAS BORN IN 1669 AND DIED IN 1767,
THEY LIVED IN THE SEVEN SUCCESSIVE REIGNS OF
CHARLES II,
JAMES II,
WILLIAM AND MARY,
QUEEN ANN,
GEORGE I,
GEORGE II
AND HIS PRESENT MAJESTY,
TO PERPETUATE THEIR MEMORY,
AND THE SINGULAR INSTANCE OF THEIR
LONGEVITY AND DEPARTURE IN
THE SAME YEAR OF THEIR AGE,
THIS TABLET WAS ERECTED BY THEIR
AFFECTIONATE NEPHEW,
THEOPHILUS DAVYES GARENCIERES.

A tribute to longevity: east wall of south aisle, St. Helen's.

1733; the bones were removed to a small site in Davygate.

The church is first mentioned in 1235 and the present building is mainly 13th and 14th-century work with a west front by William Atkinson (1875) — apparently not much changed from what was there before. The building was nearly demolished in 1548, and again in 1910, but survives to serve an active congregation.

Formerly this was the glass painters' church — many

43

and Elizabeth (1669-1767) Davyes' memorial was erected by their nephew, Theophilus Davyes Garencieres whose own monument on the north wall reveals that he died in St. Domingo, of yellow fever, 10 January, 1797, in his 31st year and was buried there with military honours.

*The York Blue Coat Boys School used St. Anthony's Hall from 1705 until 1946. The Hall is now part of the Borthwick Institute of Historical Research.

St. Helen: (or Helena) lived about 250-330 and was a Roman empress who was converted to Christianity about 312. On a pilgrimage to Jerusalem she found what she believed were relics of the True Cross. She seems to have been one of the earliest Christian archaeologists and was the mother of Constantine who was proclaimed emperor here in York in 306 A.D. (He subsequently became the first Christian emperor).

Some 135 churches were dedicated to her, mainly in the North-east, no doubt as a result of the connexion between Constantine and York.

HOLY TRINITY, Goodramgate

It is usually possible to escape from the crowds in Low Petergate into the tranquility of Holy Trinity Church and churchyard by means of a narrow passage called Hornpot Lane, on the left as you walk from the Minster towards King's Square. If the gate is locked entrance is by way of the fine 18th-century arch, with 19th-century iron work, a short distance along Goodramgate, by the side of Lady Row.

Holy Trinity is the least restored of the York churches, but this is not to say it is neglected, redundant though it is. The building is in the care of the Redundant Churches Fund and a custodian, and there is an active Association of the Friends of Holy Trinity; the church is used for worship several times a year, notably on Trinity Sunday — the Sunday after Pentecost.

18th-century gateway; 15th-century tower; 14th-century shops or Lady Row; 60-72 Goodramgate.

Holy Trinity is first mentioned in 1082, but its fittings — which give the church its distinctive appearance — are mainly 18th-century work — the Communion rail, 1715, the reredos, 1721 (painted for £10 by a Mr. Horsley), a two-decker pulpit 1785, and pews from 17th-19th centuries. Arthur Mee said, over 50 years ago, 'here everything is crazy, but clean and quaint and captivating'; this is still true.

Holy Trinity, Goodramgate: characteristic York communion rail — by John Headlam, 1715.

44

There is a squint in the South Chapel of St. James which gave a glimpse of the elevation of the Host at Mass celebrated at the high altar. The east window with its double representation of the Holy Trinity (centre light) was given by the rector, John Walker, in 1470.

The 15th-century tower has a tiled saddleback roof, which is unusual in York.

Lady Row (or, more properly Our Lady's Row) borders the churchyard to the south of the church and dates from 1316. Income from these dwellings originally endowed a Chantry to the Blessed Virgin Mary in Holy Trinity Church; this is one of the earliest jettied ranges in the country still surviving.

Holy Trinity: God the Three in One; The Father, the Son Jesus Christ and the Holy Spirit.

HOLY TRINITY, Micklegate

The Priory Church of the Holy Trinity stands at the top of Micklegate hill, between Trinity Lane and a range of timber-framed buildings. The churchyard is especially attractive in springtime when the early bulbs are flowering and before the trees give too much shade.

The architectural history of this church is extremely complex — even by York standards — and the present building stands on a Roman site. The church existed before the Norman Conquest and was known as 'Holy Trinity in the Suburbs'. As a Priory church it was refounded in 1089 but since then has been partially demolished and then added to. The tower does not even properly belong to Holy Trinity Church but was that of an adjacent church of St. Nicholas. The chancel was built in 1887 (by Fisher and Heppel) and the west front — visible from Priory Street — between 1902 and 1904 by Hodgson Fowler.

The east and west windows have fine glass by C. E. Kempe, there is a handsome font cover (18th-century) — originally in St. Saviour's — and there are fine monuments (some from St. John's, now the Arts Centre). The memorial (right, at entrance to the chancel) to Dr. John Burton who died in 1771

Holy Trinity, Micklegate: reconstructed west front and tower, from Priory Street.

commemorates the original 'Dr Slop' of Sterne's *Tristram Shandy* who was an ardent Jacobite and friend of Flora MacDonald.

The churchyard contains the parish stocks, and nearby is Jacob's Well, a medieval timber-framed house. This was the home of two chantry priests before the Reformation, and after the dissolution of the Priory it became the home of the last Prioress of St. Clement's

nunnery, Dame Isobella Ward. In the 19th century the house was an inn and became a church property again in 1905. It is now a parish room and has undergone extensive restoration during 1991.

Holy Trinity: see Holy Trinity, Goodramgate.

The former ST. JOHN, Micklegate

The former church of St. John stands at the junction of Micklegate and North Street. The church was closed in 1934 but subsequently restored by the Civic Trust and used as an Institute of Advanced Architectural Studies. It is now the Arts Centre which houses an intimate theatre (seating 100 at present, although it is hoped to increase capacity to 150), a small restaurant and a tiny exhibition area.

The first mention of this church was in 1194. The tower of the church was blown down in 1551 and the present modest tower of brick and timber replaced it in 1646. The stained glass was removed to York Minster

Above: St. John's, Micklegate, from the south-east: the unexpectedly 'rural' tower is visible.

Top left: Jacob's Well, Trinity Lane. The railings have recently been replaced by more attractive bollards.

Bottom left: Holy Trinity, Micklegate: the parish stocks.

in 1936, a late-15th century lectern went to All Saints, Upper Poppleton and a 17th-century font cover to St. Hilda's, Tang Hall; only a monument to Richard Yorke, a 15th-century Lord Mayor of York, remains.

St. John: was one of Christ's Twelve Apostles, probably 'the beloved disciple' and the man behind the Fourth Gospel. He was a fisherman, the brother of James bar Zebedee and is usually represented as the youngest of the Twelve. He was exiled to Patmos during Domitian's persecution and died, late in the 1st century, at Ephesus. He is sometimes represented by an eagle, sometimes with a chalice from which a serpent is emerging. The figure of St. John often appears in representations of the crucifixion together with that of the Blessed Virgin Mary.

KINGDOM HALL OF JEHOVAH'S WITNESSES, Trinity Lane

Trinity Lane and St. Martin's Lane are consecutive turnings off Micklegate, and near their junction with

Entrance and prow-like end of the Kingdom Hall of Jehovah's Witnesses.

The well-lit interior of the Kingdom Hall: the text over the platform is changed annually.

Fetter Lane and the Bishophills, Senior and Junior, stands the brick-built Kingdom Hall of Jehovah's Witnesses which serves (at present) three congregations. It was built in the then fashionable style in 1961 and occupies an irregular-shaped piece of ground in this rather neglected area of the city. The entrance with a small library leads to the main hall, off which there is a neatly furnished classroom. The structure rests on 8ft-9ft piles and is clearly efficiently and tastefully maintained.

(During 1992 two of the three congregations will migrate to a new Kingdom Hall to be built in one weekend at Huntington, a suburb of York.)

The former LENDAL CONGREGATIONAL CHAPEL, Lendal

Lendal House, almost opposite the Judges' Lodging in Lendal, is now occupied by a restaurant and other enterprises. The ground-floor elevation gives no indication that this was formerly an Independent Chapel opened in November, 1816, to seat nearly 1,000 persons at a cost of £3,000. Later an extra gallery was added and the total cost of £4,200 was paid off by 1837.

J. P. Pritchett's Lendal Congregational Chapel, 1816.

This was the first chapel in York to be lit by gas lamps. The upper part of the frontage more clearly indicates the building's original purpose. J. P. Pritchett was the architect and, for more than half a century, a leading member of the congregation. The chapel closed in 1920.

James Pigott Pritchett 1789-1868

James Pritchett, the architect of Lendal Chapel, could have claimed with some justification to have changed the face of York in the first half of the 19th century. A mere list of his buildings, not all surviving, indicates the variety and scale of his undertakings: Lendal Chapel, 1816, the Old Deanery, 1827-31 (demolished late 1930s), the Savings Bank, St. Helen's Square (with C. Watson), 1829-30, St. Peter's (now the Minster) School, 1832, the Cemetery Chapel, Fulford 1837, the houses facing the west front of York Minster 1838-9, Salem Chapel, 1838 (demolished 1960s), the new Lady Hewley's Almshouses, 1840, and Ebenezer Chapel, 1851. In addition he was a staunch upholder of Independency, from the period between 1814 and 1822 when York had no Independent pastor, through the heady days when Lendal Chapel in 1837 had evening congregations of over 1,100 people and nearly 450 members, until the Congregationlists began to run out

An early signed photograph of architect J. P. Pritchett.

(*York Minster Library*)

of steam in Lendal (although they continued to thrive in the newer Salem Chapel) in mid-century.

Pritchett was a deacon for half a century — not always to the satisfaction, one imagines, of pastors who came and went rather frequently between 1844 and 1869 after a succession of disagreements with their deacons.

Brick tower and disused Norman doorway of St. Margaret's, Walmgate.

St. MARGARET, Walmgate

St. Margaret's used to be one of the hidden churches of York, rather like Holy Trinity, Goodramgate, but the demolition of buildings in Walmgate and the rather half-hearted planting of shrubs leave this neglected churchyard open to all. The fine wrought-iron gateway by the York iron-founder Walker survives but now excludes nothing and nobody.

The church, at present closed and used as a theatre store, was first mentioned in the 12th century. The attractive brick tower dates from 1684. The principal attraction, however, is the Norman doorway — the finest of the three in this part of York — placed here after St. Nicholas's was destroyed in 1644. General Fairfax, preserver of the stained glass in York Minster during the Civil War, is said to have done this.

19th-century cast-iron gateway by Walker's of York whose foundry was also in Walmgate.

Capital (probably restored) on colonnette of Norman doorway — St. Margaret's.

St. Margaret: (of Antioch) probably never actually existed, and her cult was suppressed in 1969. She was popular, nonetheless, in the Middle Ages, as the patron saint of childbirth, and over 200 churches were dedicated in her name. St. Margaret is said to have been swallowed by a dragon (which subsequently burst and delivered her!) and she is sometimes represented with this beast.

The Shrine of St. Margaret Clitherow: 35 Shambles.

ST. MARGARET CLITHEROW, Shambles

No 35, Shambles is a dark, discreet and unobtrusive shrine to St. Margaret Clitherow (or Clitheroe) and was at one time believed to be the house she occupied until her martyrdom im 1586. Expert opinion now claims No. 10, on the oppposite side of the street, as her home in which she sheltered a Jesuit priest. She was put to death under a door on which was heaped heavy stones; she was canonised in 1970. The oratory was furnished

Gilded statue of St Margaret Clitherow.

by the Catholic Women's League, after the property was renovated between 1957 and 1960; Mass is now celebrated in the shrine regularly. Statues of St. Margaret Clitherow and Blessed Thomas Thwing, a native of Heworth, who was the last priest to be hanged drawn and quartered, in 1680, stand in niches behind the altar.

St. MARTIN-CUM-GREGORY, Micklegate

The rather gloomy looking church of St. Martin-cum-Gregory stands back off the road at the foot of Micklegate hill in a dank churchyard. This is another of York's redundant churches, used now as a Mothers' Union Centre and for charitable fund-raising events. It has to be said that these excellent activities do little for the appearance of a church which has much of interest to the visitor.

The church is mentioned in Domesday Book and has re-used Roman stone in the tower which was rebuilt in 1844. St. Gregory's Church was demolished in Elizabethan times and the parish united with St. Martin's.

St. Martin's has some notable furnishings — not always seen to best advantage in the midst of jumble — a pulpit of 1636, altar rails of 1753 (the typical York arrangement of three-sided enclosure with a semi-circular gate), a reredos of similar date, bread shelves, poor box and font cover.

William Peckitt (1731-95) is buried in the chancel and a window painted by his wife commemorates this important York glass painter. Henry Gyles (1645-1709), another glass painter is buried in the churchyard. Another window, by Peckitt, is a memorial to his daughters. The east window of the south aisle, about 1340, depicts St. Martin flanked by Our Lady and St. John.

Two quarries have scratched inscriptions expressing good Hanoverian sympathies — 'I hope this may be a place for true protestants to resort and never be ruled by Papists. God Bless King George ye 2d. and Billy of Cumberland whome God long preserve' and 'Our

St. Martin-cum-Gregory: Brick tower (rebuilt 1844).

Noble Duke Great Georges Son who Beat ye Rebels near Culloden the 16th Day of April 1746.'

St. Martin: see St. Martin-le-Grand, Coney Street.

St. Gregory: c.540-604. Gregory the Great was the Pope who sent St. Augustine to convert the Anglo-Saxons in 597. Known as 'the Servant of the servants of God', he is associated with Gregorian Chant, or plain song. 32 ancient churches were named after him.

ST. MARTIN-LE-GRAND, Coney Street

St. Martin-le-Grand is in Coney Street, not far from the Mansion House, and almost opposite the entry into New Street. The church can be identified at a distance by the large clock on an enormous 19th-century cast-iron bracket which overhangs the busy pedestrian street. The clock is surmounted by the figure, which survives from an earlier clock, of the 'little Admiral' who points his sextant at the sun. The original clock was placed here in 1668; the present clock is a replacement after the 1935-45 war by Mr. G. Newey of York.

The church, mentioned in the Domesday Survey, was heavily restored in 1872 and severely damaged by enemy action in 1942 — the only York church to have this melancholy distinction. It was partially rebuilt by Mr. George Pace 1961-68, the restored south aisle becoming the church and the remainder a memorial garden. The highly coloured new ceiling to the south

Above: St. Martin-le-Grand from a 19th-century engraving.
(York Minster Library).

Above right: 'Last Supper' by Frank Roper, was intended for the reredos, but not used as such.

Bottom right: Font cover (1717) surmounted by the Dove representing the Holy Spirit.

52

The restored south aisle of St. Martin's is now the whole church.

ST. MARY, Bishophill Junior

St. Mary, Bishophill Junior, is a secluded church, well away from the main tourist trails, but easily located from Priory Street or Trinity Lane — both off Micklegate. The church is probably of pre-Conquest foundation and the late Saxon tower (possibly just post-Conquest) has re-used Roman stones in it. The tower arch may actually be Roman too, but at any event this is the oldest church architecture in York. It is likely

aisle aroused critical comment when it was first seen, and the distinctive case for the new organ (itself a German gift) was also designed by Mr. Pace. The 1717 font cover is the finest in the City and Harry Stammers' modern east window is noteworthy, but the greatest treasure is the St. Martin window, given in 1437 by Robin Semer, Chamberlain to the Chapter of York. Originally the west window, the post-war restoration re-sited it in the north wall, at a lower level. The donor is depicted below a large figure of St. Martin of Tours, the patron saint of the church, scenes from whose life fill the rest of the window.

St. Martin: c.316-397 was a Hungarian soldier who became a monk and, in 372, Bishop of Tours. He was credited with miracles in his lifetime, and legend says that whilst still a soldier he shared his cloak with a beggar who was ultimately revealed to him as Jesus Christ. This scene is depicted on the lamp-posts in the parish of St. Martin-in-the-Fields in London. In England over 170 churches were dedicated to St. Martin who is often depicted with a globe of fire over his head as he celebrates Mass. His other attribute is a goose — perhaps because his feast day (11 November) is at the season of the migration of geese.

The oldest church building in York: the tower of St. Mary, Bishophill Junior.

St. Mary, Bishophill Junior: 14th-century south aisle.

Bishophill: probably indicates that this land hereabouts belonged at some time to the Bishop of York.

The former ST. MARY, Castlegate

The former church of St. Mary, Castlegate, now 'The York Story' (formerly The Heritage Centre) stands between the Jorvik Exhibition and Fairfax House, and houses an excellent collection of models, artefacts, display panels and audio-visual presentation which neatly complements the more specialised attractions of its neighbours. The 152-foot spire of the church (York's tallest) can be seen readily from the Castle car

that the tower served as the nave of the original church — perhaps with a small eastern arm: today its base has been converted into a useful room which may claim to be the most ancient in the city. The church has undergone alteration in every century from the 12th to the 17th, and a substantial restoration in 1860.

Inside are preserved part of the shaft of a Saxon cross, a strange series of almost triangular arches in the south aisle (14th-century) a fine oak font lid (17th/18th-century), a little 15th-century glass in one window, royal arms of George III (1793) painted on canvas, and a reredos and pulpit of 1889 by Temple Moore, recently suitably recoloured and gilded.

This homely, almost rural-seeming, church breathes an atmosphere of prayer.

There was, formerly, a St. Mary, Bishophill Senior, but this church was demolished in 1963 and features from it were incorporated into the modern church of Holy Redeemer, Boroughbridge Road. The sculptor Flaxman, born whilst his parents were visiting York, was baptised in St. Mary, Bishophill Senior.

St. Mary: The Blessed Virgin Mary, Mother of Jesus Christ, Son of God. More churches are dedicated to Our Lady than to any other saint.

The dedication stone of (probably) St. Mary's, Castlegate, is unfortunately undated.

park, as well as from St. Mary's Square — part of the Coppergate development which overlays what was St. Mary's churchyard, said to be the burial place of Father Thomas Thwing, hanged, drawn and quartered in 1680 for alleged conspiracy against Charles II.

The first church here was built about 1020 and a Saxon dedication stone still exists stating that it was built by 'Efrard, Grim and Aese', and referring to it as a 'mynster'.

The present building is mainly Perpendicular in style, much restored by Butterfield in 1868-1870 and adapted and skilfully remodelled within, 1974-1975. A mezzanine has been created at the east end of the building and the exit is via the space once occupied by the east window of the south aisle. The attractive re-use of a redundant church in this way was one of the first of its kind and many will feel that it is highly successful. The architects were Pace and Sims.

St. Mary's spire — the tallest in York — from the multi-storey car park.

The former ST. MICHAEL, Spurriergate

The former church of St. Michael, now the Spurriergate Centre, stands at a busy road junction, on the corner of Ousegate and Spurriergate. It houses an excellent café, a shop selling Third World goods, and an advice centre under the auspices of St. Michael-le-Belfrey Church.

The church is first mentioned in 1088 but since then has undergone constant change and restoration. Rebuilt in the 1820s and again in the 1860s, the church has lost half a bay. The tower all but disappeared in the 1960s when it was lowered, in consequence of failure to

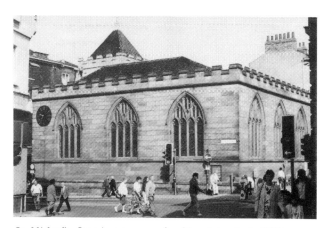

St. Michael's, Spurriergate, was refaced in gritstone in the 1800s.

St. Michael, Spurriergate: 12th-century columns; 18th-century altar piece surmounted by St. Michael; 20th-century restaurant.

discern any foundations. The interior, however, beautifully restored by George Pace in 1965 and sympathetically modified since, is probably the most attractive of all York's churches. The elegant 12th-century columns, the splendid 15th-century south aisle glass with the Nine Orders of Angels window, and the handsome early 18th-century altar rails, reredos and door case combine to produce a lovely effect.

Other delights include the annealed coloured glass 'jewels' in St. John's robe in the south-east window, a chalice brass to a 15th-century rector, William Langton (1466) (only three others in Yorkshire), and the memorial (by Fisher) to William Hutchinson who died in 1772.

ST. MICHAEL-LE-BELFREY

St. Michael's stands close to the south-west tower of York Minster (hence 'le-Belfrey') on a piece of ground bounded by Petergate, Minster Yard and Minster Gates.

A church on this site is mentioned at the end of the 13th century but tradition says the church was first built in 1066. The present building is the largest of the old City churches and dates from the time of Henry VIII. It is the last pre-Reformation church to have been built in the City; the west front, however, was rebuilt in 1867.

St. Michael's contains interesting stained glass — the east window is 14th-century glass from an earlier church — a splendid altar piece which cost £68 in the 18th century; the former altar stone from the Minster, set in the floor of the nave; 17th-century brasses; 18th-

St. Michael-le-Belfrey (from the belfry of York Minster) built by John Forman, 1525-1536.

Reredos and altar rails, 1712, by William Etty.

1821. He was also Vicar of Huntington 1789-1802 and in charge of St. Sampson's from 1802 until his death. For the last 18 years of his life he was also Sub-chanter at the Minster. During this period he supervised the cataloguing of the Minster Library — for which he was paid ten guineas —, compiled the York Psalm and Hymn Book, tended those imprisoned in York Castle and founded the York Sunday School Committee and the York Charitable Society. Above all, he filled St. Michael's with a huge congregation necessitating the addition in 1785 of the gallery, and all this at the time of the growth of Methodism which in York arose out of the evangelical revival within the Church of England. Relations were such that it is said the Wesleyans of Peasholme Green Chapel were accustomed to attend

century monuments, including a handsome one to Robert and Priscilla Squire, attributed to John Nost and Andrew Carpenter; mayoral boards from 1711, 1804 and 1808 and a copy of the following entry in the parish register (now in the Minster Library) 'Christeninges 1570: Guye Fawke sone to Edward Fawke the XVI day of aprile'.

St Michael's has a western gallery, but lacks a chancel as such. It is, however, a suitable building for a large and vigorous congregation which was built up by the late Revd. David Watson (died 1984), formerly at St. Cuthbert's and later at St. Michael's. The congregation at the end of the 18th century experienced a similar revival under William Richardson who served St. Michael's from 1771 to 1821.

The Revd. William Richardson (1745-1821)

William Richardson was a vicar choral of York Minster and in charge of St. Michael-le-Belfrey from 1771 until

Engraving of William Richardson 1745-1821.   (*York Minster Library*)

57

St. Michael's for Holy Communion after their own preaching service, during the ministry of William Richardson.

He was buried at St. Michael's and his memorial is on the east wall of the north aisle.

The Revd. David Watson (1933-1984)

David Christopher Knight Watson was educated at St. John's College and Ridley Hall, Cambridge. He came to Heworth Parish Church, York, in 1965 and was put in charge of St. Cuthbert's which was at that time on the brink of redundancy with a mere handful of

David Watson, Vicar of St. Michael-le-Belfrey, 1973-1984.

worshippers. In less than a year, as a result of David Watson's preaching and teaching based on the Gospel and the power of the Holy Spirit, the church was full to overflowing. The evangelical revival was continued when in 1973 the congregation moved to the largest of the city's churches, St. Michael-le-Belfrey, and David Watson became vicar. St. Michael's too, had only a small but faithful congregation at this time, so another city-centre church was saved from redundancy by the injection of new Spirit-filled life and once again pews and gallery were filled. David Watson's charismatic ministry spread from York to university missions and became known in many places overseas. He also managed to write a number of books and broadcast on radio and television, communicating the Gospel to thousands until his untimely death in 1984.

St Michael: one of the Archangels of Hebrew tradition. The name means 'Who is like God?' and Michael appears in the Books of Daniel and Revelation as the leader of God's heavenly army against the forces of evil, usually represented by a dragon.

St. Wilfrid is said to have had a vision of St. Michael prior to his death and nearly 700 medieval churches were dedicated to him. St. Michael was regarded as the patron of cemeteries and is sometimes represented as weighing souls at the Last Judgement, sometimes slaying a dragon.

The former MONK BAR CHAPEL, Goodramgate

The Monk Bar Chapel of the York United Methodist Free Church Circuit was built at a total cost of £3,100 in 1859 near the junction of Aldwark and Goodramgate. It is of red and white brick and was built to accommodate 800 people. The chapel changed hands in 1907, and in 1919 became the Monk Bar Central Mission. This closed in 1934 and the chapel was sold for £1,850.

In recent years the property has been used by a wholesale tobacconist. Now one end of the building is

The former Monk Bar Chapel, Goodramgate, has lost its portico.

ST. OLAVE, Marygate

St. Olave's in Marygate (off Bootham) is the exception in this catalogue of places of worship within the City walls: it is in fact within the walls of St. Mary's Abbey — indeed the north wall of the church was part of the Abbey's defences. The church can be approached by way of the Museum Gardens and lies beyond the ruins of the Abbey Church.

St. Olave's (locally prounounced Olive's), was founded by Siward of Northumbria (mentioned in *Macbeth*) who died about 1055. The *Anglo-Saxon Chronicle* records that 'he lieth at Galmanho, in the minster that he had had built and hallowed in God's name and Olaf's'. (Galmanho was the name of the settlement outside the city walls in the Marygate area). Although originally within the Abbey precincts it was used as a parish church. The present building is mainly Perpendicular, rebuilt in 1721-2 with additions in 1879 (the chancel, by George Fowler Jones), 1895 (the vestry) and 1908 (south chapel). The roof was used as a gun platform during the siege of York in the Civil War (1644). The east window has fragmentary medieval glass showing Gabriel and Our Lady; there are also five saints including (fourth from the left) Olaf. A small

St. Olave's from the south-east. The tower was restored in 1991.

divided into three — a gift shop, a turf accountant's and a clothes shop; the other end of the building contains the Judges' rooms and the bailiffs' rooms. The premises used to have a portico over the entrance, and besides the chapel included classrooms, schoolrooms, vestries and caretaker's house and a tea room!

window by Harry Stammers depicts the Annunciation (1957), and the Victorian font has a cover designed by George Pace (1963).

Two monuments are of interest — one, inside the church to William Thornton 'Joyner and Architect' who died in 1721 (he helped save the north transept of Beverley Minister from collapse in 1716, and also probably worked at Beningbrough Hall); the other, south of the church by a doorway in the wall of the ruined Abbey Church, to the York artist, William Etty, died 1849, whose statue stands outside the Art Gallery in Exhibition Square.

St. Olave (or Olaf): 995-1030 was King of Norway from 1016 to 1029. He was converted to Christianity in England, fighting the Danes, but himself used force to make Norway Christian. He was deposed and defeated in battle but rehabilitated as patron saint of Norway. Over 40 churches are dedicated in his name, mainly in areas under Viking influence.

William Etty, R.A. (1787-1849)

William Etty, the son of a miller, was born in York in 1787. Apprenticed at the age of eleven to a letterpress printer in Hull, he later in 1806 went to London and studied at the Royal Academy schools and, for a year, under Sir Thomas Lawrence. In 1811 his first painting was hung in the Royal Academy. Later he travelled and painted in Italy, but from 1826 until 1848 he lived in London. In 1828 he became a Royal Academician but still continued to attend life classes. In 1848 he returned to York and died the following year.

His paintings are primarily of classical, Biblical and historical subjects with such varied titles as 'Benaiah, one of David's Mighty Men', 'Robinson Crusoe returning thanks to God for his deliverance' and 'Female bathers surprised by a swan'. The National Gallery possesses twelve canvases, including 'Youth on the Prow, and Pleasure at the Helm' —Etty's pictures have a self-confessed moral dimension – and the York Art Gallery also has a considerable collection, many of which are on public display. Etty had a great love of his

The statue of William Etty, R.A., stands outside the City Art Gallery in Exhibition Square.

native city and played a prominent part in the conservation of its antiquities.

His statue stands in Exhibition Square and his tomb in St. Olave's churchyard can be seen from the ruins of St. Mary's Abbey, although the inscription can only be read from the churchyard.

The former PEASHOLME GREEN CHAPEL

Where Aldwark joins St. Saviour's Place at Peasholme Green stands the earliest surviving Methodist chapel in York.

The oldest surviving Methodist Chapel in York: the Peasholme Green Chapel, now a dental surgery.

In 1753 John Wesley had preached at 'room in Pump Yard', which he referred to as an oven, and the following year the building which stood at the junction of Newgate and Patrick Pool was registered as a place of worship. (This building was rebuilt in 1963). In 1759 the building at the end of Aldwark with about 400 seats was the scene for another sermon by Wesley on 19 April. In 1775 another 100 seats were added.

In 1806 the Chapel was sold for £530 and the upper floor became a hayloft and the lower was divided into four tenements. Later the building was used as a warehouse; today it is a dental surgery.

PRIORY STREET BAPTIST CHURCH

Entering Priory Street from Micklegate, the Baptist Church is on the right behind cast-iron railings, painted blue. This was the first Nonconformist church in York to be built in the neo-Gothic style in 1868. The architect was William Peachey of Darlington whose very different Victoria Bar (Primitive Methodist) Chapel is not far away. William Peachey was much employed by the railway companies, having a hand in Middlesbrough and York Central Stations. He also was the architect for the Station Hotel, York, (now Royal York Hotel), completed in 1878. Here he used stone for the front and ends of the church but brick at the back. The tower, sadly, was lowered in the 1920s and the manse (shown on the water colour in the vestry) was never built.

The interior, with delicate cast-iron columns and wrought-iron capitals, is light and attractive; the gallery has white painted panels with a rose design. The interior of the chapel was remodelled and reduced in size at the outset of World War II, and restoration work is in progress now (1992). The pastor of the church between 1872 and 1874 was Frederick Brotherton Meyer who invited the American evangelist D. L.

York Baptist Church in Priory Street with its truncated tower (extreme right).

William Peachey's original design for the Baptist Church, daringly Gothic in 1868.

Moody to preach in Priory Street. I. D. Sankey sang at these evangelistic gatherings and 'touched men's hearts'. The leather-topped table (which incorporates a wash bowl) around which the leaders of the mission prayed in 1873 and from which 'the river of blessing for

This plaque, in Newgate Market, predates the many excellent Civic Trust plaques elsewhere in York.

the whole country has sprung' is preserved in the chapel and is something of a relic — especially for American visitors.

The former 'ROOM IN PUMP YARD', Newgate-Patrick Pool

In 1753 John Wesley preached in what was called 'the room on Pump Yard' and the following year, 1754, the place was registered for Methodist worship. Wesley referred to the upper room in which meetings were held as 'the oven'. The premises were rebuilt in 1963 and little remains of the original fabric.

The former ST. SAMPSON

The former church of St. Sampson presides over the busy thoroughfare of Church Street, between Patrick Pool and Silver Street (until 1991 part of the open air market). First mentioned in 1152 the church was much rebuilt between 1440 and 1450 and again in 1848.

By 1968 St. Sampson's was redundant and closed. In 1974, under the guidance of George Pace and Ronald Sims, with funds from the Hayward Foundation (£65,000) the church was converted into a social centre for the elderly.

The outward appearance of the church remains virtually unchanged. Inside a mezzanine floor over the north aisle gives office space, and the former sanctuary has been converted into a small chapel in which services are held regularly. Kitchen facilities are in the south aisle and the former parish room has been annexed. Some 1,500 elderly people use the centre daily from Tuesday until Saturday. On Mondays the building is used for fund-raising events.

The west window has one panel of medieval glass, there is a brass memorial to William Richardson (signed by Joshua Mann) and the reredos in the Chapel incorporates painted panels by Bodley from the now demolished church of All Saints, Scarborough. There are notable roof bosses in the nave, restored and recoloured in 1974.

St. Sampson's.

St. Sampson: is said to have been the founder of the church over 800 years ago. The saint is not to be confused with the Sampson of the Old Testament and he may, or may not, have been the St. Sampson, a Celtic saint, who became Bishop of Dol in the 6th century. Attempts to make him a bishop of York before Paulinus are unconvincing and his connection, if any, with York remains a mystery.

The Revd. H. N. V. Tonks (1881-1959)

Horace Norman Vincent Tonks, educated at Walsall Grammar School and Lichfield Theological College, was ordained during World War I and saw service in Belgium. After the war he served in parishes in Scarborough and Hull and as Vicar of St. Sampson's with Holy Trinity from 1926 until 1935. During this time he was active in Anglo-Catholic affairs, as Northern-area Secretary for the Anglo-Catholic Congress and overseas Secretary of the Church Union. In 1936 he was consecrated Bishop of the Windward Islands and worked unceasingly for his West Indian people until ill health made him retire in 1949. For a few years he returned to England but returned in 1956 to Castries, St. Lucia, as rector, where he died three years later.

Two sons followed him into the priesthood and his 'missus' (as he called her), Alice, was a constant support to him.

He is still remembered with affection for his wit and humour, his love of children and his staunch support for Catholic faith and practice.

Father Tonks, as he was in 1919.

The former ST. SAVIOUR

Half hidden behind Stonebow House, at the junction of Hungate and St. Saviourgate stands the former church of St. Saviour, now the Archaeological Resource Centre. The only Anglican church in this enclave of Nonconformity, this building founded at least as early as 1090, was redundant and unloved for many years. In 1988 it began its new life under the care of the York Archaeological Trust.

In medieval times it was known as 'St. Saviour in the Marsh' — the River Foss being less well organised in those days. The 15th-century tower stands in interesting contrast to the Ionic portico of the Central Methodist Church — both showing their superiority to the concrete car park which obtrudes nearby. St. Saviour's was largely rebuilt in 1844-1845 by R. H. Sharp, and modified internally between 1986 and 1987. A mezzanine floor at the level of the capitals occupies the aisles and west end of the building, giving room for research facilities; the ground floor is devoted to educational and storage uses. The vault is richly coloured — rose madder and green — as a reminder of the glorious decoration of medieval church interiors.

St. Saviour: Saint, derived from the latin *'Sanctus'*, here means Holy, so 'the Church of the Holy Saviour' (i.e. Jesus Christ, Redeemer of Mankind).

The Archaeological Resource Centre now occupies St. Saviour's Church. The bridge links the mezzanines of south and north aisles.

The former SKELDERGATE MISSION

The derelict red-brick building at the corner of Queen's Staith Road and Skeldergate is the sad remnant of a vigorous Wesleyan mission built in 1900 for £2,852. The hall accommodated 300 people.

This mission had previously been conducted from premises in North Street; these were subsequently taken over by the Salvation Army in 1905.

Services were held at the mission on Sundays and considerable social work was done from this centre; as many as 10,000 dinners were given to poor children during the winter of 1907-8. The mission closed in 1939.

In December, 1942, the building was re-opened as King George VI's Club for Officers and since 1955 has been used by Remploy Ltd. and a commercial firm. At present (1992) the building stands empty.

Skeldergate Mission at the end of 1991. The Mission's hall was lit by the large window on the right.

The former TRINITY CHAPEL, Peckitt Street

Tower Street does a right-angled bend at the point it meets Clifford Street; Peckitt Street joins them here and runs down to the South Esplanade. (Peckitt Street is named after the 18th-century York glass painter, William Peckitt.)

At the south end of the Fire Station is the Byzantine-style front of J. B. and W. Atkinson's Trinity Chapel, built in 1856 for the Methodist New Connexion, and used by this body until 1907.

In 1935 the Chapel was sold and converted — if that is the word — to an extension for the Fire Station.

Polychrome brick on the facade of the former Trinity Chapel. The square-headed windows are a later intrusion.

UNITARIAN CHAPEL, St. Saviourgate

Beyond the Central Methodist Chapel and St. Saviour's Church (now the Archaeological Resource Centre), towards the Spen Lane end of St. Saviourgate, stands the oldest of York's Nonconformist churches. The Unitarian Chapel of brick, cruciform with a central tower and shallow pitched slate roof, was built for the Presbyterians in 1693. Lady Sarah Hewley was the chief patron of the Chapel and also endowed almshouses (originally in Tanner's Moat but from 1840 on the other side of St. Saviourgate).

The church became Unitarian in 1756. The chapel was restored in 1991 — twice — at a cost of some £170,000 and the re-decorated interior is decorous and pleasant. The excellent pews have been painted 'sequoia' red. There are fine monuments, a Georgian pulpit and — in the vestry — Lady Hewley's chair and a copy of a portrait of the Revd. Charles Wellbeloved who ministered here from 1792 until 1858. This

The Unitarian Chapel built on a Greek-cross plan in 1693. There were, formerly, windows in the central tower.

Lady Sarah Hewley (1627-1710)

Lady Sarah Hewley was the wife of John Hewley (1619-1697) who was recorder for Doncaster. Knighted in 1663 and M.P. for York 1678, 1679 and 1681. She was buried, as was her husband, in St. Saviour's and had a house in St. Saviourgate. Lady Sarah was the benefactress of the Presbyterian Chapel (now Unitarian) in St. Saviourgate, the Almshouse (1700) which bears her name, and the York Charity Schools (1705) founded by Archbishop Sharpe.

She also left income for 'poor and godly preachers for the time being of Christ's holy gospel'. Her portrait and

Gates and railings by the Walmgate foundry of Walker's of York, in St. Saviourgate.

ministry must have been notable, even in an age of lengthy tenures: at all events Charles Wellbeloved was buried just outside the sanctuary of the chapel he served with such distinction.

The handsome railings (1852) are by the Walker foundry of York and replace a brick wall which in earlier times repulsed the unsympathetic.

Portrait of Lady Sarah Hewley which hangs in the entrance hall of the Mansion House.

Lady Sarah Hewley's chair, in the vestry of the Unitarian Chapel.

that of her husband are the property of the Unitarian Chapel but hang in the entrance hall of the Mansion House.

The Revd Charles Wellbeloved (1769-1858)

Charles Wellbeloved was brought up by his grandfather and was known to John Wesley; he grew up to be a prominent Unitarian divine and archaeologist. He came to York in 1792 initially as an assistant minister, but from 1800 until 1858 he was the senior minister of the Unitarian Chapel. In 1803 the Manchester Academy moved to York and Wellbeloved

was its director until 1840; a student described his teaching as 'candid and catholic, simple and thorough'. His public spirit made him a founder of the Subscription Library (1794), the Philosophical Society (1822), and the York Institute (1827), as well as the School of Design, the Savings Bank and the Cemetery Company.

Memorial to Charles Wellbeloved, his wife and daughter. The cryptic original is above.

Charles Wellbeloved. Minister 1792-1858, from a portrait in the vestry.

The asymmetric façade of William Peachey's Primitive Methodist (Victoria Bar) Chapel of 1880.

He wrote much, including books on the archaeology of York. He also assisted in raising funds for the restoration of the Minster after the 1829 fire, and he successfully opposed a plan to remove the choir screen.

His portrait was painted by James Lansdale in 1826: a copy hangs in the St. Saviourgate Chapel's vestry.

VICTORIA BAR CHAPEL, Victor Street

The prominent building of red and white brick with terracotta dressings in a so-called 'Renaissance' style, which stands at the junctions of Victor Street and Newton Terrace was a chapel built for the Primitive Methodists at a cost of over £3,500 and opened in 1880. The architect was W. Peachey of Darlington who also designed the Baptist Chapel in Priory Street. It was

closed and sold in 1940 and has since served as a furniture store.

The curious asymmetrical exterior of the chapel seems little changed, but inside, a reinforced upper floor has obliterated the gallery, leaving only the handsome cast-iron columns which supported it visible.

During 1991 the Chapel was re-opened as the Church of the Redeemer by a charismatic free church. The offices of the Cephas Trust are also here: the Cephas Trust is a registered charity which aims to provide accommodation for disadvantaged young people between the ages of 16 and 25.

ST. WILFRID, Duncombe Place

Of all the York churches the Roman Catholic church of St. Wilfrid is the easiest to find: like St. Michael-le-Belfrey it cannot be misssed by the visitor seeking the Minster. Situated in Duncombe Place, the dominant

George Goldie's splendid tower for St. Wilfrid's Roman Catholic Church on its awkward site between hotel and theatre.

Interior of St. Wilfrid's.

priest at St. Wilfrid's Mission. The church occupies an awkward site between the stage door of the Theatre Royal and the Dean Court Hotel. St. Wilfrid's was the cathedral for the diocese of Beverley but lost its status when the diocese was absorbed into those of Leeds and Middlesbrough. The interior is both impressive and cold due to the unusual high dark vault and restrained colours — particularly of the Whitby sandstone with which the church is lined. The 'sumptuous sanctuary fittings' have not succumbed to the recent re-ordering so the impression given to a former director of the Warham Guild of a 'superior soda fountain' remains. Nevertheless there is a good deal of interest here and familiarity breeds increasing respect.

St. Wilfrid: 634-709. Wilfrid was educated at Lindisfarne, Canterbury and Rome. He became Bishop of York but had connections also with Ripon (where he was buried), Hexham, Sussex, Frisia and Lyons. A repeated visitor to Rome, he was also an apostolic pioneer, a founder of monasteries, a builder of churches, a patron of art and the champion of the Roman Church versus the Celtic. His attributed arms are three gold suns on a blue background.

tower and ornate west portal built in the late 13th-century French Gothic style are visible from Museum Street, challenging the photographer to take a picture of the west front of the Minster without them.

The church was built between 1862 and 1864 to designs by the architect George Goldie who was born round the corner in St. Leonard's; his brother was a

YORK MINSTER

The largest Gothic church in Northern Europe, with a nave seating 2,000 people, has been the subject of so many books that it seems foolish to attempt even a mere paragraph in such a survey as this. 'The cathedral and metropolitical church of St. Peter in York' — more commonly known as *the* Minster — has been visited by the famous (and the infamous) as well as the obscure throughout its long history, so perhaps it can be

Early 19th-century engraving of York Minster, from Hargrove's New Guide.

summed up in the words of Sarah, Duchess of Marlborough, who in 1732 opined: 'a gothic building, the finest I ever saw, a vast deal of what they call architecture, which is no where so well as in a church'.

St. Peter: originally a fisherman, brother of Andrew and the leader of the Twelve Apostles. He was the first to acknowledge Jesus as the Messiah or Christ and was entrusted with 'the keys of the Kingdom of heaven' (hence his symbol). Nicknamed 'the Rock', he denied knowing Jesus thrice before the cock crowed on the first Good Friday. After the resurrection he was charged by the risen Lord to 'Feed my Sheep' and tradition makes him the first Bishop of Rome. He is said to have been crucified upside down.

York Minster: West front with the 'Heart of Yorkshire' window.

Books Consulted

The Buildings of England — Yorkshire: York and the East Riding, N. Pevsner.

Victoria County History — York.

Bartholomew City Guides — York, J. Hutchinson and D. M. Palliser.

A Short History of the Baptists in York 1646-1987, R. R. Darsley.

St. Columba's United Reformed Church — One Hundred Years 1873-1973, F. H. Legg.

The Penguin Dictionary of Saints, D. Attwater.

The Oxford Dictionary of Saints, D. H. Farmer.

Medieval York, A. Raine.

Dictionary of National Biography.

A History of St. Wilfrid's Mission, York, D. Minskip.

Eric Milner-White — a memoir, P. Pare and D. Harris.

St. Michael-le-Belfrey, Lion Pocket Guides.

Collins Guide to English Parish Churches, J. Betjeman (Ed.).

Nonconformity in Nineteenth-Century York, E. Royle.

York College for Girls:
Detail from the Annunciation window by Harry Stammers.

York Minster, almost devoid of scaffolding, soars above the city, the Mother church of the diocese and Northern province.